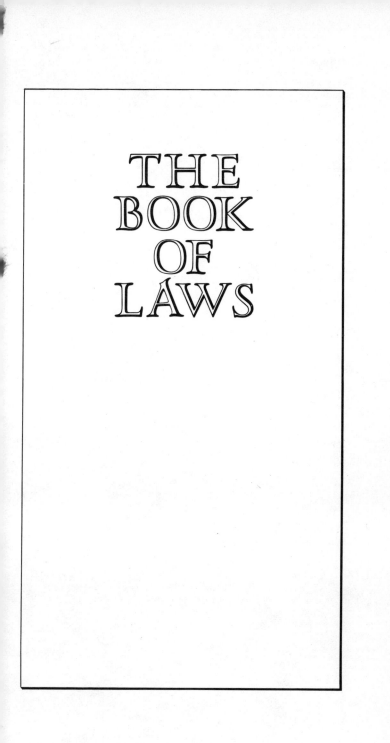

THE
BOOK
OF
LAWS

THE BOOK OF LAWS

HAROLD FABER

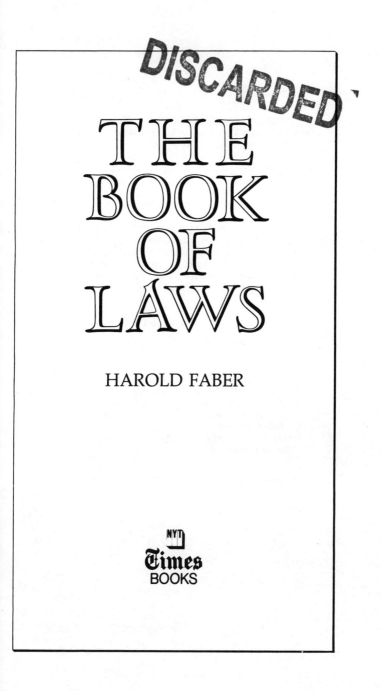

NYT
Times
BOOKS

Published by TIMES BOOKS, a division
of Quadrangle/The New York Times Book Co., Inc.
Three Park Avenue, New York, N. Y. 10016

Published simultaneously in Canada by
Fitzhenry & Whiteside, Ltd., Toronto

Library of Congress Cataloging in Publication Data

Main entry under title:

The Book of laws.

  1. Social systems—Quotations, maxims, etc.
  2. Social systems—Anecdotes, facetiae, etc.
  3. Social psychology—Quotations, maxims, etc.
  4. Social psychology—Anecdotes, facetiae, etc.
  I. Faber, Harold.
  HM51.B728   1979   301   78-19608
  ISBN 0-8129-0728-0

Manufactured in the United States of America

CONTENTS

Introduction   vii

Chapter 1   The Laws of Behavior   3
Chapter 2   The Laws of Bureaucracy   17
Chapter 3   Laws for Consumers   31
Chapter 4   The Laws of Culture and Art   43
Chapter 5   The Laws of Economics   53
Chapter 6   The Laws of Government   63
Chapter 7   The Laws of the Media   75
Chapter 8   The Laws of Politics   83
Chapter 9   The Laws of Science   91
             and Technology
Chapter 10   The Laws of Sports   101
Chapter 11   The Laws of Everything Else   107

INTRODUCTION

The birth of the modern era of law discoverers, who should not be confused with elected lawmakers, can be pinpointed precisely. On November 19, 1955, Professor C. Northcote Parkinson published an article in the staid pages of *The Economist* of London about a law that he had discovered while investigating the British Admiralty and the Colonial Office: *Work expands to fill the time available for its completion.*

Instantly, Parkinson's Law was universally acknowledged as a basic truth that transcended all national borders, with worldwide implications for all bureaucracies—in fact, all organizations. It was accepted without reservation as part of our cultural and scientific heritage, just as valid as Newton's three laws of motion. Parkinson became famous, while disciples by the score followed his example and discovered other laws—some original, some derivative, some funny, some descriptive, some merely aphorisms.

Meanwhile, another seminal law, even more basic than Parkinson's, was quietly spreading by word of mouth, first among missile engineers, then designers and technicians, and in technical journals. Murphy's Law—*if anything can go wrong, it will*—was embraced by the scientific and engineering community, and then by almost everybody.

But who was Murphy? For a quarter of a century or more, his law was attributed to an unknown Murphy, but recently one claimant has been put forth. In a book, appropriately enough called *Murphy's Law*, a letter is presented from an engineer in California, citing a remark by a "Captain Ed Murphy," otherwise unidentified, at a missile test laboratory back in 1948 as the genesis of Murphy's Law. However, that letter is dated 1977. It seems strange that during a thirty-year period, with Murphy's Law being constantly quoted in engineering circles, that the real Murphy, if there ever was one, has not stepped forward. Not proven would seem to be the best verdict at this time, and so, among law experts, Murphy's Law is still the child of an unknown Murphy.

However, by another name, the same law was being discovered at about the same time by another researcher, who called it Chisholm's Law, which, unfortunately for his fame and fortune, did not have the same melodious ring as Murphy's Law. Like a Mozart developing a theme and its variations, Francis O. Chisholm, who toiled in relative obscurity as chairman of the Department of English at the Wisconsin State University—River Falls, explored what he called the laws of frustration, mishap, and delay. His three laws and their several corollaries, first published in *Motive* magazine and then as a chapter of *A Stress Analysis of a Strapless Evening Gown and Other Essays for a Scientific Age* in 1963, are masterpieces of descriptive analysis.

Like most modern developments, the new art of discovering laws has ancient roots, starting when Moses came down from the Mount with his laws, the Ten Commandments. Archimedes leaped from his bathtub crying "Eureka!" when he produced his law, sometimes called Archimedes' Principle—*that a body immersed in water displaces its own weight*. Back in the sixteenth century, Thomas Gresham discovered the law that bears his name—*bad money drives out the good*—a law that obviously is universally true.

As the age of science blossomed, natural laws were

observed everywhere: the laws of reflection and re-
fraction, the law of diminishing returns, the law of
original horizontality, the laws of thermodynamics,
the law of optics. Many of them were, and are,
anonymous, but some were honored with the name of
the discoverer. In school, some of us still learn about
Kepler's Laws, Mendel's Laws, Faraday's Laws,
Charles' Law, Boyle's Law, Newton's Laws, and
scores of others, even though we may know little
about the discoverers themselves.

To them we are now adding hundreds of new laws
and names, derived from the current renaissance of
law discovery. Some of the new names are known;
some are not. Some may turn out to be footnotes in
history; some will live on as long as their laws are
cited. As an aid to future historians, I have tried to
trace the origins of the laws cited in the following
pages.

But there has been a vast amount of misquotation,
appropriation of ideas (and sometimes the actual
wording of the laws themselves), mislabeling, and
confusion. In my early days of law collecting, dating
back twenty years, I failed to keep accurate notes of
the origins of some laws, although I faithfully clipped
all that I could find. Also, I have tried to use original
sources, but have been forced to rely on secondary
sources in some cases, which led some years back to
the promulgation of Faber's Law: *The number of errors
in any piece of writing is directly proportional to the
amount of reliance on secondary sources.* And so, if there
are any errors in this collection, I apologize in advance.

Some general observations about discovered laws
should be made as a guide to the pages that follow.
Most of the modern laws bear the names of their
discoverers, which is only proper recognition of their
perspicacity. Some unskilled practitioners label their
discoveries "iron" or "immutable" or "first," as if

that adjectival nomenclature adds to the inherent truth, which is not so. Others affix higher numbers to their laws, as if "sixth law" or "eighth law," for example, is more true than merely a law, which is not necessarily so.

The rigorous standards for accurate classification of a discovery as a law include, foremost, an insight that is instantly recognizable to all, with universal application. Like a scientific theory, it must stand up against further observation and testing. Moreover, a law must be succinct, elegantly expressed, and bear the name of its discoverer. I must admit, however, that some anonymous laws, some laws with numerical prefixes, and even a few "principles" and "maxims" have been admitted to this collection.

By the highest of the above standards, Parkinson, Murphy, and Chisholm can justly be called the founding fathers of law discovery, a trinity that stands preeminent in the field. Their names will surely live along with those of Newton, Malthus, Kepler, Gresham, Mendel, Ohm, and Einstein.

Will any of the others in the following pages become household words? If I had to pick one that has the potential to become a classic, it would be Weiler's Law: *Nothing is impossible for the man who does not have to do it himself.* It was named for and by Abe Weiler, who spent part of his career as a movie critic and movie editor observing his senior editors at *The New York Times*.

As the careful reader may note, many of these laws come out of the pages of *The New York Times*, mostly because I worked there for so many years and read its pages so carefully. But I have used other sources as well, collecting laws for years and writing about them. My first article on laws was published on the editorial page of *The Times* back in 1962, and subsequent collections have appeared in *The New York Times Sunday*

Magazine (in 1968) and more recently in *The Times* Travel Section.

For help beyond the usual, I want to thank my wife, Doris; my daughters, Alice and Marjorie; other collectors in the field; and, above all, my friend, classmate, and colleague, Alan L. Otten, the distinguished political columnist of *The Wall Street Journal,* whose annual column of laws delights readers of that newspaper.

HAROLD FABER

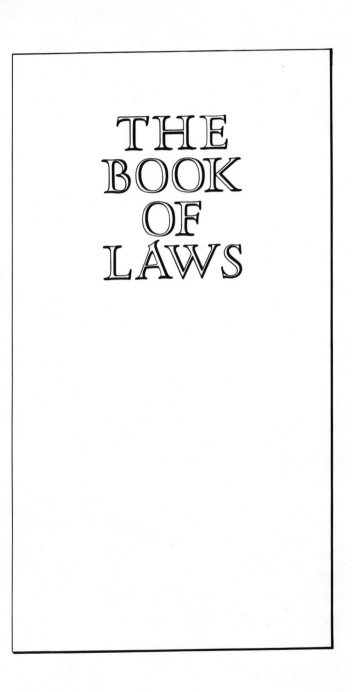

THE
BOOK
OF
LAWS

CHAPTER ONE

THE LAWS OF BEHAVIOR

TO BE HUMANIZED IS TO
COMPLY WITH THE TRUE LAW
OF OUR HUMAN NATURE.
Matthew Arnold

THE FIRST LAW OF ANIMAL APPEAL
The popularity of an animal is directly correlated with
the number of anthropomorphic features it possesses.

THE SECOND LAW OF ANIMAL APPEAL
The age of a child is inversely correlated with the size
of the animals it prefers.
> (Desmond Morris, in *The Naked Ape*,
> McGraw-Hill, 1967.)

ANNENBERG'S LAW
No good deed will go unpunished.
> (Walter Annenberg, quoted in Ann Lan-
> ders' column, in *The Poughkeepsie Journal*,
> March 26, 1978. Also attributed to Clare
> Booth Luce, in *Playboy*, April 1978.)

BERGER'S LAW
Difficult situations are most often easier to get into
than out of.
> (Emanuel Berger, in a letter to the author,
> 1968.)

BERNSTEIN'S FIRST LAW
A falling body always rolls to the most inaccessible
place.
> (Theodore M. Bernstein, in *The Careful
> Writer*, Atheneum, 1967.)

BOK'S LAW
If you think education is expensive, try ignorance.
> (Derek Bok, quoted by Ann Landers, in
> *The Poughkeepsie Journal*, March 26, 1978.)

BOOKER'S LAW
An ounce of application is worth a ton of abstraction.
(Quoted in *Murphy's Law*, by Arthur Bloch,
Price/Stern/Sloan, 1977.)

CARVER'S LAW
The trouble with radicals is that they read only radical
literature, and the trouble with conservatives is that
they don't read anything.
(Thomas Nixon Carver, quoted in *The New
Republic*, March 28, 1970.)

CHESHIRE'S LAW OF SOCIAL CLIMBING
Everything that goes up must come down.
(Maxine Cheshire, in *Life*, February 28,
1969.)

CHISHOLM'S FIRST LAW OF HUMAN
INTERACTION
If anything can go wrong it will.

CHISHOLM'S FIRST COROLLARY
If anything just can't go wrong, it will anyway.

CHISHOLM'S SECOND LAW
When things are going too well, something will go
wrong.

CHISHOLM'S SECOND COROLLARY
Any time things appear to be going better, you have
overlooked something.

CHISHOLM'S THIRD LAW
Purposes, as understood by the purposer, will be judged otherwise by others.

Corollaries
1. If you explain so clearly that nobody can misunderstand, somebody will.
2. If you do something which you are sure will meet everybody's approval, somebody won't like it.
3. Procedures devised to implement the purpose won't quite work.

> (Francis P. Chisholm, in "The Chisholm Effect," in *Motive* magazine, and then in *A Stress Analysis of a Strapless Evening Gown and Other Essays for a Scientific Age*, Prentice-Hall, 1963.)

THE TEN COMMANDMENTS
1. Thou shalt have no other gods before Me.
2. Thou shalt not make unto thee any graven image.
3. Thou shalt not take the name of the Lord thy God in vain.
4. Honor thy father and thy mother.
5. Thou shalt not kill.
6. Thou shalt not commit adultery.
7. Thou shalt not steal.
8. Thou shalt not bear false witness against thy neighbor.
9. Thou shalt not covet thy neighbor's house.
10. Thou shalt not covet thy neighbor's wife, nor his manservant, nor his maidservants, nor his ox, nor his ass, nor anything that is thy neighbor's.

> (*The Bible*, The Book of Exodus.)

COUDERT'S LAW
Love is not only changed by observation, it is changed for the worse.

> (Jo Coudert, in *Advice from a Failure*, Stein and Day, 1965.)

ERVIN'S LAW
When two men communicate with each other by word of mouth, there is a twofold hazard in that communication.

> (Sam Ervin, at the Watergate hearings, quoted in *The New York Times*, July 13, 1973.)

FETRIDGE'S LAW
Important things that are supposed to happen do not happen, especially when people are looking, or, conversely, things that are supposed not to happen do happen, especially when people are looking.

> (Claude Fetridge, quoted in H. Allen Smith's *A Short History of Fingers*, Little, Brown, 1963.)

THE FIFTH RULE
You have taken yourself too seriously.

> (An unknown British diplomat, quoted by John Chancellor, and requoted in *The Wall Street Journal*, March 3, 1974.)

FORRESTER'S LAW (1)
In complicated situations, efforts to improve things often tend to make them worse, sometimes much worse, on occasions calamitous.

> (Jay W. Forrester, quoted in *The New York Times*, June 4, 1971.)

FORRESTER'S LAW (2)
In a complex social system, the obvious, common-sense solution to a problem will turn out to be wrong most of the time.

> (Jay W. Forrester, quoted in *The New York Times*, October 16, 1971.)

GILHOOLEY'S PRINCIPLE
As a guide to events, if not to conduct, no amount of cynicism is excessive; you cannot err on the high side.
> (Quoted in a letter to the author from John F. Hellegers, March 19, 1968.)

ONE OF THE FIRST LAWS OF GNOMERY
Gnomes always draw curtains where there are views.
> (Ada Louise Huxtable, in *The New York Times*, November 16, 1975.)

THE FIRST GNOMIC LAW
The outrage of sacrificing trees and the park-edge promenade is to be inflicted where it will do the most damage and attract the least attention.

THE SECOND GNOMIC LAW
Once you have your foot in the asphalt, you can finish what you have started.

THE THIRD GNOMIC LAW
There is no time like a gas shortage with an uncertain traffic and transportation future to widen Fifth Avenue, if it were desirable to widen Fifth Avenue under any circumstances, which it is not.
> (Editorial, *The New York Times*, April 4, 1974.)

GOMPERTZ'S LAW
The chance of dying doubles about every eight years, irrespective of the environment in which one lives.
> (Benjamin Gompertz, quoted in *Natural History*, February 1973.)

GUMPERSON'S LAW
The frequency of the occurrence of an event is inversely proportional to its desirability.
> (Quoted in *Changing Times*, November 1957.)

HALL'S LAW
The higher a person's social position, the more names he is likely to have.
> (Quoted in *The Saturday Review*, February 1, 1964.)

HANSEN'S AXIOM
What the son wishes to forget, the grandson wishes to remember.
> (Marcus Lee Hansen, quoted in *Newsweek*, July 4, 1977.)

HARDIN'S LAW
You can never do merely one thing.
> (Garrett Hardin, quoted in *Fortune*, February 1973.)

THE FIRST LAW OF HERO-DYNAMICS
Every epic action has an equal and opposite reaction.
> (*Time*, July 23, 1973.)

HERRNSTEIN'S LAW (1)
The attention paid to an instructor is a constant regardless of the size of the class; thus, as the class swells, the amount of attention paid per student drops in direct ratio.
> (Richard Herrnstein, quoted by Alan L. Otten, in *The Wall Street Journal*, December 28, 1973.)

HOWE'S LAW
Every man has a scheme that won't work.

> (Quoted by Alan L. Otten, in *The Wall Street Journal*, February 20, 1975.)

THE LAWS OF HUSKING
The laws of husking every wight can tell —
  And sure no laws he ever keeps so well:
For each red ear, a general kiss he gains.

> (Joel Barlow, 1754–1813, in *Hasty Pudding*.)

THE LAW OF INVERSE PROPORTION
OF SOCIAL INTERCOURSE
The possibility of a young man meeting a desirable and receptive young female increases by pyramidal progression when he is already in the company of (1) a date, (2) his wife, (3) a better-looking and richer male friend.

> (Ronald Beifield, quoted by Alan L. Otten, in *The Wall Street Journal*, February 2, 1975.)

SOME ISSAWI LAWS OF SOCIAL MOTION

The Law of Conservation of Evil
The total amount of evil in any system remains constant. Hence any diminution in one direction—for instance a reduction in poverty or unemployment—is accompanied by an increase in another, e.g., crime or air pollution.

The Course of Progress
Most things get steadily worse.

The Path of Progress
A shortcut is the longest distance between two points.

The Dialectics of Progress
Direct action produces direct reaction.

On Reform
Most people do not go to the dentist until they have a toothache; most societies do not reform abuses until the victims begin to make life uncomfortable to others.
> (Charles Issawi, in *The Columbia Forum*, Summer 1970.)

THE ISSAWI-WILCOX PRINCIPLE
Problems increase in geometric ratio, solutions in arithmetic ratio.
> (Ibid.)

JARVIS' LAW
Admissions to state mental hospitals vary positively with geographic proximity.
> (Quoted by Alex D. Pokorny, in *The Houston Post*, November 30, 1975.)

JENKINSON'S LAW
Everybody's crazy.
> (Quoted in *The New Republic*, circa 1970.)

JONES' LAW
Friends may come and go, but enemies accumulate.
> (Thomas Jones, quoted by Alan L. Otten, in *The Wall Street Journal*, February 20, 1975.)

MC LAUGHRY'S CODICIL TO JONES' LAW
To make an enemy, do someone a favor.
> (James McLaughry, quoted by Alan L. Otten, in *The Wall Street Journal*, February 20, 1975.)

THE LAWS OF THE JUNGLE
Now these are the laws of the jungle
  And many and mighty they are;
    But the head and the hoof of the Law
      And the haunch and the hump is —
        Obey.

> (Rudyard Kipling, 1865–1936, in "The Law of the Jungle.")

KELLEY'S LAW
Last guys don't finish nice.

> (Stanford Kelley, quoted by Alan L. Otten, in *The Wall Street Journal*, February 26, 1976.)

KRISTOL'S LAW
Being frustrated is disagreeable, but the real disasters of life begin when you get what you want.

> (Irving Kristol, quoted in *Newsweek*, November 28, 1977.)

LAKEIN'S LAW
There's always time enough for the important things.

> (Alan Lakein, quoted in *The Wall Street Journal*, December 17, 1969.)

LIEBLING'S LAW
If you try hard enough, you can always manage to boot yourself in the posterior.

> (A. J. Liebling, quoted in *The New York Post*, September 9, 1968.)

LIPPMANN'S LAW
When all think alike, no one is thinking.

> (Walter Lippmann, quoted by Ann Landers, in *The Poughkeepsie Journal*, March 26, 1978.)

MARTIN'S THEORY
No matter what occurs, there is always someone who believes it happened according to his pet theory.

> (J. M. Martin, quoted in *Industry Week* magazine.)

MESKIMEN'S PRINCIPLE
There's never time to do it right, but always time to do it over.

> (John Meskimen, quoted by Alan L. Otten, in *The Wall Street Journal*, March 14, 1974.)

MIDAS' LAW
Possession diminishes perception of value, immediately.

> (John Updike, in *The New Yorker*, November 3, 1975.)

MONDALE'S LAW
If you are sure you understand everything that is going on, you are hopelessly confused.

> (Walter Mondale, quoted by Ann Landers, in *The Poughkeepsie Journal*, March 26, 1978.)

PAUL'S LAW
When others experience us differently than we think
they should, this usually has the effect of making us
conclude that other people are either hostile or not
understanding.
>   (Norman Paul, quoted by William J. Le-
>   derer, in *New York* magazine, circa 1974.)

PETERSON'S THEORY OF INTERLOCKING
NEUROSES
The rocks in my head fill the holes in yours.
>   (Peter G. Peterson, quoted in *Fortune*,
>   March 1973.)

PIETROPINTO'S PETER PAN PRINCIPLE
Marriages peter out or pan out.
>   (Anthony Pietropinto, M.D., in *Husbands
>   and Wives*, Times Books, 1979.)

PRICE'S LAW
If everybody doesn't want it, nobody gets it.
>   (Quoted in an ad by Atlantic Monthly Press
>   Books, in *The Atlantic*, March 1969.)

RILEY'S LAW
To get anything, you have to have something.
>   (Quoted from *The Life of Riley*, by Anthony
>   Cronin, Knopf, 1964, in *The New York
>   Times Book Review*, May 24, 1964.)

RUDIN'S LAW
In a crisis that forces a choice to be made among alternative courses of action, most people will choose the worst one possible.

> (S. A. Rudin, in a letter to *The New Republic*, 1961.)

SCHONBERG'S LAW
Anybody who gets away with something will come back to get away with a little bit more.

> (Harold Schonberg, in *The New York Times*, October 8, 1972.)

SPOCK'S LAW
Kids will, over the long run, eat what their bodies demand, providing their parents will let them alone.

> (Benjamin Spock, quoted by George Herman, CBS News, December 2, 1971.)

GEORGE'S COROLLARY TO SPOCK'S LAW
Mothers obviously will never leave kids alone when it comes to eating what said mothers have lovingly cooked for them; and faced with unhappy mothers, fathers will add their bit of pressure.

> (George Herman, CBS News, December 2, 1971.)

TORQUEMADA'S LAW
When you are right, you have a moral duty to impose your will upon anyone who disagrees with you.

> (Quoted by Alan L. Otten, in *The Wall Street Journal*, September 18, 1977.)

TREEMAN'S LAW
Every activity takes more time than you have.

> (Quoted in The *Farmers' Almanac*, 1978.)

TRISTAN'S LAW
Appealingness is inversely proportional to attainabil-
ity.

> (John Updike, in *The New Yorker*,
> November 3, 1975.)

TRUE FRIENDSHIP'S LAW
Welcome the coming, and speed the parting guest.

> (Alexander Pope, 1688–1744, in *The Odys-
> sey of Homer*.)

WEST'S LAW
Sooner or later, everything becomes too important for
someone else to handle.

> (Dick West, in *The Hudson Register-Star*,
> October 20, 1975.)

THE FIRST LAW OF WING-WALKING
Never leave hold of what you've got until you've got
hold of something else.

> (Quoted by Alan L. Otten, in *The Wall
> Street Journal*, September 18, 1977.)

THE LAW OF THE YUKON
That is the law of the Yukon, that only the strong shall
  thrive,
That surely the weak shall perish, and only the fit
  survive.

> (Robert W. Service, 1874–1958, in "The
> Law of the Yukon.")

CHAPTER TWO

THE LAWS OF BUREAUCRACY

THERE IS ONLY ONE GIANT MACHINE
OPERATED BY PYGMIES,
AND THAT IS BUREAUCRACY.
Honoré de Balzac

ACHESON'S RULE OF THE BUREAUCRACY
A memorandum is written not to inform the reader but to protect the writer.

> (Dean Acheson, quoted by Alan L. Otten, in *The Wall Street Journal*, September 18, 1977.)

THE FUNDAMENTAL LAW OF ADMINISTRATIVE WORKINGS (F.L.A.W.)
Things are what they are reported to be. Or, the real world is what is reported to the system. Or, if it isn't official, it hasn't happened.

> (John Gall, in *Systemantics*, Quadrangle/ The New York Times Book Co., 1977.)

THE IRONCLAD RULES FOR SUCCESSFUL ADMINISTRATION
1. If a program doesn't work, expand it.
2. The bigger it gets, the less notice anyone will take that it isn't working.

> (Robert Schrank, in *Ten Thousand Working Days*, MIT Press, 1978.)

BERLE'S FIVE LAWS OF POWER
1. Power invariably fills any vacuum in human organization.
2. Power is invariably personal.
3. Power is invariably based on a system of ideas or philosophy.
4. Power is exercised through, and depends on, institutions.
5. Power is invariably confronted with, and acts in the presence of, a field of responsibility.

> (Adolf A. Berle, in *Power*, Harcourt Brace, 1969.)

BOREN'S LAWS
1. When in charge, ponder.
2. When in trouble, delegate.
3. When in doubt, mumble.
>   (James Boren, quoted in *Time*, November
>   23, 1970.)

BUCY'S LAW
Nothing is ever accomplished by a reasonable man.
>   (Fred Bucy, quoted in *Malice in Blunder-
>   land*, by Thomas L. Martin, Jr., McGraw-
>   Hill, 1973.)

THE LAWS OF BUREAUCRATIC IMMOBILITY
1. Never do anything for the first time.
2. Pay is a function of the time spent.
3. Wait till others have given clearance.
4. It is futile, so why try.
5. Make only big mistakes.
>   (Byron L. Johnson, in *The Washington Post*,
>   October 22, 1972.)

THE BUREAUCRATIC TEN COMMANDMENTS
1. Don't discuss domestic politics on issues involv-
   ing war and peace.
2. Say what will convince, not what you believe.
3. Support the consensus.
4. Veto other options.
5. Predict dire consequences.
6. Argue timing, not substance.
7. Leak what you don't like.
8. Ignore orders you don't like.
9. Don't tell likely opponents about a good thing.
10. Don't fight the consensus and don't resign over
    policy.
>   (Leslie H. Gelb and Morton M. Halperin, in
>   *The Minneapolis Star and Tribune;* in
>   *Harper's*, June 1972; and in *The Washington
>   Post*, August 6, 1972.)

DILWETHER'S LAW OF DELAY
When people have a job to do, particularly a vital but
difficult one, they will invariably put if off until the
last possible moment, and most of them will put it off
even longer.

> (Gordon Becker, quoted by Alan L. Otten,
> in *The Wall Street Journal*, February 26,
> 1976.)

DOW'S LAW
In a hierarchal organization, the higher the level, the
greater the confusion.

> (Quoted by Laurence J. Peter, in *The Peter
> Prescription*, William Morrow, 1972.)

ERB'S EDICT
Regardless of output, an "operator" can rise indefinitely.

> (Guy F. Erb, quoted in *The National Ob-
> server*, September 23, 1972.)

GAMMON'S LAW
In a bureaucratic system, increase in expenditure will
be matched by fall in production.

> (Max Gammon, quoted by Milton Fried-
> man, in *Newsweek*, November 7, 1977.)

THE LAW OF GROWTH
Systems tend to grow, and as they grow, they en-
croach.

> (John Gall, in *Systemantics*.)

HENDRICKSON'S LAW
If you have enough meetings over a long enough
period of time, the meetings become more important
than the problem that the meetings were intended to
solve.

> (E.R. Hendrickson, quoted in *Malice in
> Blunderland.*)

HUXTABLE'S IMMUTABLE LAW
All autonomous agencies and authorities, sooner or
later, turn into self-perpetuating strongholds of con-
ventional thought and practice.

> (Ada Louise Huxtable, in *The New York
> Times,* August 22, 1971.)

IMHOFF'S LAW
The organization of any bureaucracy is very much like
a septic tank; the big chunks always rise to the top.

> (Attributed to John Imhoff, in *Malice in
> Blunderland.*)

ISSAWI'S FIRST LAW OF
COMMITTO-DYNAMICS
Comitas comitatum, omnia comitas.

ISSAWI'S SECOND LAW OF
COMMITTO-DYNAMICS
The less you enjoy serving on committees, the more
likely you are to be pressured to do so.

> (Charles Issawi, in *The Columbia Forum,*
> Summer 1970.)

A THIRD LAW OF COMMITTO-DYNAMICS
The amount of useful accomplishment, U, achieved
by people working on a committee is approximated

by $U = n/2n-1$. Thus, if one or two people produce a unit of useful work, three will produce three-quarters of a unit, four one-half of a unit and so forth.

> (Harmon H. Goldstone, in a letter to *The New York Times*, January 18, 1971.)

A RURAL NEW ENGLAND VERSION OF THE THIRD LAW

One boy helping, a pretty good boy; two boys, half a boy; three boys, no boy.

> (Quoted by Margaret Follett, in a letter to *The New York Times*, January 31, 1971.)

KIRKLAND'S LAW

The usefulness of a meeting is in inverse proportion to the attendance.

> (Lane Kirkland, quoted by Alan L. Otten, in *The Wall Street Journal*, March 3, 1974.)

LE CHATELIER'S PRINCIPLE

Complex systems tend to oppose their own proper function.

> (Henri-Louis Le Chatelier, 1850–1936, quoted in *Systemantics*.)

LEEDS' LAW OF RED TAPE

Time required to process paper is the sum of the number of agencies or levels involved, squared.

> (Morton Leeds, in a letter to the author, March 20, 1968.)

A LIVING LAW OF SOME PUBLIC SERVANTS
How much can we get away with.
> (Alan Dershowitz, in *The New York Times Book Review*, October 31, 1971.)

THE MC NAUGHTON RULE
Any argument worth making within the bureaucracy must be capable of being expressed in a simple declarative sentence that is obviously true once stated.
> (John McNaughton, quoted by Alan L. Otten, in *The Wall Street Journal*, March 3, 1974.)

MARTIN'S LAW OF COMMUNICATION
The inevitable result of improved and enlarged communication between different levels of a hierarchy is a vastly increased area of misunderstanding.
> (Thomas L. Martin, Jr., in *Malice in Blunderland*.)

METZ'S LAW
Being the boss doesn't make you right, it only makes you the boss.
> (Milton Metz, in a letter to the author, March 23, 1968.)

MILES' LAW
Where you stand depends on where you sit.
> (Rufus Miles, quoted by Elliot Richardson, in *The New York Times Magazine*, May 20, 1973.)

NADER'S AXIOM
The speed of exit of a civil servant is in direct proportion to the quality of his service.
> (Ralph Nader, quoted in *The Washington Post*, October 30, 1970.)

THE NEWTONIAN LAW OF
SYSTEMS INERTIA
A system that performs a certain function or operates in a certain way will continue to operate in that way regardless of the need or of changed conditions.
> (John Gall, in *Systemantics*.)

NIES' LAW
The effort expanded by a bureaucracy in defending any error is in direct proportion to the size of the error.
> (John Nies, quoted by Alan L. Otten, in *The Wall Street Journal*, December 20, 1973.)

O'BRIEN'S LAW
At some time in the life cycle of virtually every organization, its ability to succeed in spite of itself runs out.
> (Richard O'Brien, quoted in *Malice in Blunderland*.)

PARKINSON'S LAW
Work expands to fill the time available for its completion.
> (C. Northcote Parkinson, in *The Economist*, November 19, 1955.)

PARKINSON'S SECOND LAW
Expenditure rises to fill income.
> (C. Northcote Parkinson, in *The Law and the Profits*, Houghton Mifflin, 1960.)

PARKINSON'S THIRD LAW
Growth leads to complexity, complexity to decay.
> (C. Northcote Parkinson, in *Inlaws and Outlaws*, Houghton Mifflin, 1962.)

PARKINSON'S FOURTH LAW
Delay is the deadliest form of denial.
> (C. Northcote Parkinson, in *The Law of Delay*, Houghton Mifflin, 1971.)

THE PARKINSON LAW FOR CONSULTANTS
The more you use, the more you need to solve the problem.
> (Sanford D. Garelik, quoted in *The New York Times*, March 23, 1971.)

BROWN'S VERSION OF
PARKINSON'S LAW
The volume of paper expands to fill the available briefcases.
> (Edmund Brown, quoted by Alan L. Otten, in *The Wall Street Journal*, February 26, 1976.)

A DOMESTIC EXTENSION OF
PARKINSON'S LAW
Objects expand to fill the space available.
> (Patrick Ryan, in the *Smithsonian*, May 1978.)

AN OFFICE VERSION OF
PARKINSON'S LAW
Office-space needs expand instantly to fill and then overfill all the space available.

> (*The Wall Street Journal*, January 7, 1966.)

MRS. PARKINSON'S LAWS
1. Never look at the incoming mail until you have time to read it at leisure.
2. Never answer the telephone if you are in the middle of something more important. Let it ring.
3. When disaster strikes as the result of your own agitation, stop work...sit down, collect your thoughts....Do nothing until the temperature is normal.
4. In the last resort, take a cold bath or shower and emerge in a cooler frame of mind, your agitation having gone down the drain pipe.

> (C. Northcote Parkinson, in *Mrs. Parkinson's Law*, Houghton Mifflin, 1968.)

THE PETER PRINCIPLE
In a hierarchy, every employee tends to rise to his level of incompetence.

PETER'S COROLLARY
In time, every post tends to be occupied by an employee who is incompetent to carry out its duties.

> (Laurence J. Peter, in *The Peter Principle*, William Morrow, 1969.)

PUDDER'S LAW
Anything that begins well, ends badly.

> (Quoted by Laurence J. Peter, in *The Peter Prescription*.)

THE RADOVIC RULE
In any organization, the potential is much greater for the subordinate to manage his superior than for the superior to manage his subordinate; and the maximum records in employment are not to be found in upward mobility, but stability at the rank-and-file level.

> (Igor Radovic, in *The Radovic Rule*, M. Evans, 1973.)

RANGNEKAR'S RULE OF COMMITTEE SIZE
The possibility of avoiding decisions increases in proportion to the square of the number of members on the committee.

> (Sharu S. Rangnekar, in "The Art of Avoiding Decisions," quoted in *Malice in Blunderland*.)

ROBINSON'S LAW
Civilization is doomed unless some way can be found to check the growth of bureaucracy; and the only hope for the human race is for the rate of population increase to continue to exceed that of bureaucratic growth.

> (Arthur H. Robinson, quoted in a United Press—International article, in *The Albany Times-Union*, July 6, 1975.)

ROWE'S LAW
The average executive is incompetent, indifferent, irresponsible, lazy and frequently dishonest.

> (H. T. Rowe, in a letter to *The New York Times Book Review*, September 26, 1969.)

THE LAW OF SECRETIVENESS
The less management knows and understands, the more secure the job.
> (Ivor Catt, in *The Catt Concept*, G. P. Putnam's Sons, 1971.)

SHANAHAN'S LAW
The length of a meeting rises with the square of the number of people present, and the productiveness of the meeting falls with the square of the number of people present.
> (Eileen Shanahan, quoted in *Timestalk*, house organ of *The New York Times*, 1963.)

SHANNON'S LAW OF ADMINISTRATION
What is actually happening is often less important than what appears to be happening.
> (William V. Shannon, quoted in *Malice in Blunderland*.)

TRAHEY'S LAW
Never dump a good idea on a conference table. It will belong to the conference.
> (Jane Trahey, in *The New York Times*, September 18, 1977.)

THE VECTOR THEORY OF SYSTEMS
Systems run better when designed to run downhill.

A COROLLARY TO THE VECTOR THEORY
Systems aligned with human motivational vectors will sometimes work. Systems opposing such vectors work poorly or not at all.
> (John Gall, in *Systemantics*.)

WEIL'S LAW
The first-rate man will try to surround himself with
equals, or betters if possible. The second-rate man
will surround himself with third-rate men. The
third-rate man will surround himself with fifth-rate
men.

> (André Weil, quoted in *The New York Times*, March 2, 1973.)

WILSON'S LAW
A person's rank is in inverse relation to the speed of
his speech—with the fast talkers losing out to their
slower-speaking colleagues.

> (James Q. Wilson, quoted by Alan L. Otten, in *The Wall Street Journal*, December 20, 1973.)

YANNACONE'S LAWS
1. Litigation is like a club; it's got to be used or it
   becomes a deadweight.
2. When someone shoves, shove back.
3. Civilization declines in relation to the increase in
   bureaucracy.

> (Victor Yannacone, Jr., in *Sports Illustrated*, February 3, 1969.)

CHAPTER THREE

LAWS FOR CONSUMERS

**THE PEOPLE'S GOOD
IS THE HIGHEST LAW.**
Cicero

ADLER'S LAW
Insurance policies never cover what is happening.

ADLER'S LAW OF BUDGETING
Most budgets run low by 20 per cent, except renova-
tion and vacation budgets which run low by 50 per
cent.
> (Lee Adler, quoted by Alan L. Otten, in *The
> Wall Street Journal*, September 18, 1977.)

THE LAW OF AIRPLANES
When the plane you're on is late, the plane you're
trying to catch leaves on time.
> (M. Stanton Evans, quoted by Alan L. Ot-
> ten, in *The Wall Street Journal*, February 20,
> 1975.)

ALLISON'S PRECEPT
The best simple-minded test of expertise in a particu-
lar area is the ability to win money in a series of bets
on future occurrences in that area.
> (Gordon Allison, quoted by Alan L. Otten,
> in *The Wall Street Journal*, March 14, 1974.)

APPLE'S LAW
Did you ever notice how much faster wood burns
when you personally cut and chop it yourself?
> (Quoted on *Apple's Way*, on CBS, January
> 12, 1975.)

BARNUM'S LAW
You can fool most of the people most of the time.
> (P. T. Barnum, 1810–1891.)

BILLINGS' LAW
Live within your income, even if you have to borrow
to do so.
> (Josh Billings, 1818–1885, quoted by Laurence J. Peter, in *Peter's Quotations*, William Morrow, 1977.)

BRINKLEY'S LAW
As soon as you replace a lost object, you will find it.
> (David Brinkley, quoted by Ann Landers, in *The Poughkeepsie Journal*, March 26, 1978.)

CAHN'S AXIOM
When all else fails, read the instructions.
> (Quoted by Paul Dickson, in *Playboy*, April 1978.)

CRANDALL'S LAW
All tour buses arrive at the same time.
> (Robert S. Crandall, travel editor of *The New York Times*, summarizing his travel experiences.)

DANISH'S LAW
If some is good, more is better.
> (Paul H. Danish, in a letter to the author, March 24, 1968.)

DEMO'S LAW
Everything you decide to do costs more than first
estimated.
> (Quoted in the *Farmers' Almanac*, 1978.)

DEWAN'S LAW
A late train gets later.
> (William Dewan of the Canadian National Railways, in a letter to the author, March 18, 1968.)

DIAMOND'S LAW
There is an inverse ratio between services and their
cost.
> (A. Diamond, in a letter to the author,
> March 21, 1968.)

DOOLITTLE'S LAW
After a couple of drinks, you can't tell what kind of
bourbon you are drinking.
> (Ad in *The Washington Post*, November 16,
> 1965.)

ETTORE'S LAW
The other line moves faster. This applies to all
lines—bank, supermarket, tollbooth, customs, and so
on. And don't try to change lines. The other one—the
one you were in originally—will then move faster.
> (Barbara Ettore, in *Harper's*, August 1974.)

FABER'S LAW OF THE ROAD
Every other driver is either stupid or crazy.
> (Harold Faber, in *The New York Times*, Feb-
> ruary 18, 1962.)

FELDHUSEN'S LAW
The more sophisticated the equipment, the bigger the
adjustment department needed.
> (Fred Feldhusen, Jr., quoted in *The Ban-
> kers*, Weybright & Talley, 1974.)

FIG NEWTON'S LAW
When you have been thinking all day about that box
of cookies on the kitchen shelf, someone will finish
the last cookie minutes before you get home.
> (G. O. B. Drews, in a letter to the author,
> March 20, 1968.)

FINEGAN'S SECOND LAW
If it is good and I want it, they don't make it anymore.

> (Elizabeth C. Finegan, in a letter to the
> author, March 17, 1968.)

FRAZIER'S AMMENDMENT TO MURPHY'S LAW
Good parking spaces are always on the other side of
the street.

> (Claude Frazier, quoted by Alan L. Otten,
> in *The Wall Street Journal,* September 18,
> 1977.)

HARSHAW'S LAW
Daughters can spend 10 per cent more than a man can
make in any usual occupation.

> (Jubal Harshaw, in Robert A. Heinlein's
> *Stranger in a Strange Land,* G. P. Putnam's
> Sons, 1961.)

HOLT'S LAW
Any transportation option—a freeway, a subway,
whatever, serving a large dense concentration of
people—will probably be used up to the point where
it becomes unbearable.

> (J. E. Holt, in *New York* magazine, January
> 8, 1973.)

HUXTABLE'S PARKINSON-TYPE LAW
Once you provide a super-route, you do not just speed
the already stuck cars and trucks on their way, you
acquire a lot of new traffic.

> (Ada Louise Huxtable, in *The New York
> Times,* February 2, 1969.)

LAUDERDALE'S LAW
Junk expands to overflow the storage space available.
> (Vance Lauderdale III, in a letter to the au-
> thor, March 22, 1968.)

LEVENSON'S LAW
No matter how well a toupee blends in back, it always
looks like hell in front.

LEVENSON'S SECOND LAW
Insanity is hereditary; you get it from your children.
> (Sam Levenson, quoted in *Peter's Quota-*
> *tions.*)

LEWIS' LAW
No matter how long or hard you shop for an item, after
you've bought it it will be on sale somewhere cheaper.
> (Quoted in *Murphy's Law*, by Arthur Bloch,
> Price/Stern/Sloan, 1977.)

A LAW OF LIFE
There are never as many sleds, bikes or skate boards
as there are boys.
> (*Life*, May 14, 1965.)

THE LAW OF LINES
At bank, post office or supermarket, there is one universal law which you ignore at your own peril: the
shortest line moves the slowest.
> (Bill Vaughan, quoted in *Reader's Digest*,
> July 1977.)

MAGPIES' LAWS
1. The longer one saves something before throwing it away, the sooner it will be needed after it is thrown away.
2. The more irrevocably something is discarded, the more urgently it will be needed after it is discarded.
> (James J. Caufield, in a letter to the author, March 1968.)

MARTHA'S MAXIM
If God had meant us to travel tourist class, he would have made us narrower.
> (Martha Zimmerman, a former airline stewardess, quoted by Alan L. Otten, in *The Wall Street Journal*, September 18, 1977.)

MOOERS' LAW
Any information retrieval system will tend not to be used whenever it is more painful and troublesome for a customer to have information than not to have it.
> (Calvin N. Mooers, in *Army Research and Development Newsmagazine*, February 1968.)

THE MOSES LAW
Don't eat in park concessions.
> (Named after Commissioner Robert Moses by John L. Hess, in *The New York Times*, August 10, 1973.)

AND HESS' COROLLARY
The quality of food and service is inversely proportional to the captivity of the clientele.
> (John L. Hess, in *The New York Times*, August 10, 1973.)

MURPHY'S FIRST LAW OF AUTO REPAIR
Any tool dropped repairing an automobile will roll
under the car to the vehicle's exact geographic center.

> (Myron F. Johnson, quoted by Alan L. Ot-
> ten, in *The Wall Street Journal*, March 14,
> 1974.)

THE NATURAL LAW OF MONEY
Anything left over will be needed tomorrow to pay an
unexpected bill.

> (Quoted in *Reader's Digest*, July 1977.)

OLSON'S LAW
Every time you buy something, the manufacturer
comes out the next week with an improved model for
less money.

> (Quoted in the *Farmers' Almanac*, 1978.)

PERKINS' LAW
At the moment you take your shoe off in a shoe store,
your toe will pop out of your sock.

> (Quoted in the *Farmers' Almanac*, 1978.)

THE PERVERSITY OF OBJECTS PRECEPT
If it works well, they'll stop making it.

> (Jane Otten and Russell Baker, separately,
> quoted by Alan L. Otten, in *The Wall Street
> Journal*, February 26, 1976.)

THE LAW OF RESTAURANTS
The quality of food in a restaurant is in inverse proportion to the number of semicolons and exclamation
marks on the menu.

> (*Time*, December 6, 1968.)

THE ROBINSON LAW OF RECIPE DIFFICULTY
The complexity of a recipe is inversely proportional to
the number of ingredients.
> (Delmer Robinson, in *The National Ob-
> server*, 1968.)

ROCHE'S FIFTH LAW
Every American crusade winds up as a racket.
> (John P. Roche, in *The Albany Times-Union*,
> July 14, 1978.)

ROCHE'S VERSION OF MURPHY'S LAW
If you play with anything too hard, it will break.
> (John P. Roche, in *The Hudson Register-
> Star*, April 22, 1974.)

SHEINWOLD'S LAW
When traffic halts on a four-lane highway, it's a law of
nature that the other lanes move while your lane stays
glued to the road.
> (Alfred Sheinwold, in *The New York Post*,
> March 8, 1972.)

SHULL'S LAW
Everything takes longer than it's supposed to.
> (Robert Shull, quoted in *The New York
> Times*, February 15, 1964.)

SIMMONDS' LAW
Anytime you back out of a driveway, there will always
be a car coming or a pedestrian passing by.
> (Quoted in the *Farmers' Almanac*, 1968.)

THE LAW OF STATION WAGONS
The amount of junk carried is in direct proportion to
the amount of space available.

> (Tony Hogg in *Esquire*, quoted by Alan L.
> Otten, in *The Wall Street Journal*, February
> 20, 1975.)

STURGEON'S LAW
Ninety per cent of everything is junk.

> (Quoted by Christopher Lehmann-Haupt,
> in *The New York Times*, December 9, 1970.)

THE LAW OF THE TAJ MAHAL
If a tourist attraction has achieved worldwide fame,
there must be a reason.

> (James Egan, in *The New York Times*, March
> 9, 1975.)

AN IRON LAW OF TOURISM
Natural beauty is enhanced by distance from home.

> (Harold Faber, who said it had been re-
> pealed, in *The New York Times*, April 30,
> 1978.)

THE FIRST LAW OF TRAVEL
No matter how many rooms there are in the motel, the
fellow who starts up his car at 5 o'clock in the morning
is always parked under your window.

> (Quoted in *Reader's Digest*, July 1977.)

THE LAW OF WICKEDNESS OF OBJECTS
If you drop a piece of buttered bread on the carpet, the chances of its falling with the buttered side down are in direct relationship with the cost of the carpet.

> (Henry Kissinger, quoted in *Kissinger*, by Marvin Kalb and Bernard Kalb, Little, Brown, 1974.)

CHAPTER FOUR

THE LAWS OF CULTURE AND ART

THE GREAT LAW OF CULTURE
IS TO LET EACH BECOME
ALL THAT HE WAS CREATED
CAPABLE OF BEING;
EXPAND, IF POSSIBLE,
TO HIS FULL GROWTH;
RESISTING ALL IMPEDIMENTS,
CASTING OFF ALL FOREIGN,
ESPECIALLY NOXIOUS ADHESIONS,
AND SHOW HIMSELF
IN HIS OWN SHAPE AND STATURE,
BE THOSE WHAT THEY MAY.
Thomas Carlyle

THE LAW OF ADVENTURE FICTION
A high-born Briton who wanders into the wilderness must undergo total metamorphosis before he can be let out.

> (*Time*, in a review of *A Man Called Horse*, May 11, 1970.)

ALICE'S LAW
The purpose of Presidential office is not power, or leadership of the Western World, but reminiscence, best-selling reminiscence.

> (Roger Jellinek, in *The New York Times Book Review*, March 10, 1968.)

AUDEN'S LAW
It is impossible to write religious poetry.

> (*Time*, referring to W. H. Auden, in a review of *Jesus Rediscovered* by Malcolm Muggeridge, September 26, 1969.)

BERNSTEIN'S SECOND LAW
Bad words tend to drive out good ones and when they do, the good ones never appreciate in value, sometimes maintain their value, but often lose in value, whereas the bad words may remain bad or get better.

> (Theodore M. Bernstein, in *The Careful Writer*, Atheneum, 1967.)

BOUCHER'S THIRD LAW
The microcosm repeats the macrocosm.

> (Anthony Boucher, reviewing spy novels in *The New York Times Book Review*, circa 1967.)

BRECHT'S LAW
The ideal amount of rehearsal time is always one week more.

> (John Dexter of the Metropolitan Opera, quoted in *The New York Times*, February 27, 1974, referring to Bertolt Brecht.)

BROADCASTING'S VERSION OF
GRESHAM'S LAW
Any entertainment program, no matter how bad, will outdraw any public affairs program, no matter how good.

> (Edwin Diamond, in *New York* magazine, November 24, 1975.)

THE IMMUTABLE LAW OF BROADWAY
Flops outnumber hits.

IMMUTABLE COROLLARY TO THE LAW
OF BROADWAY
Playwrights and producers keep trying.

> (The *New York Herald Tribune*, just before it folded.)

THE BUYER'S DISEASE
When you are in a position to buy something that other people want to sell—in my case manuscripts or chances of a job—you are treated with a deference beyond your desserts. When you leave your editorial chair—or as a buyer of anything—and people no longer have any material reason to cater to you, it can be a traumatic experience.

> (Bruce Bliven, former editor of *The New Republic*, in *The New Republic*, January 9, 1971.)

CATLEDGE'S LAW
Culture expands the time available for it.

> (Turner Catledge, then executive editor of
> *The New York Times*, in an internal com-
> munication, 1970.)

COHN'S LAW
It's what you listen to when you're growing up that
you always come back to.

> (Al Cohn, quoted by Nat Hentoff, in *The
> New York Times*, November 24, 1968.)

COWLEY'S LAW
No complete son-of-a-bitch ever wrote a good sentence.

> (Malcolm Cowley, in *And I Worked at the
> Writer's Trade*, Viking, 1978.)

CROSBY'S LAW
You can tell how bad a musical is by how many times
the chorus yells, "hooray."

> (John Crosby, in the *New York Herald
> Tribune*, quoted in *Playbill*, circa 1967.)

FITZ-GIBBON'S LAW
Creativity varies inversely with the number of cooks
involved in the broth.

> (Bernice Fitz-Gibbon in *Macy's, Gimbels
> and Me*, Simon and Schuster, 1967.)

GIBRAN'S LAW
The more complex the epoch, the simpler must be its

solutions. The harder the time, the softer its lit(era-ture).

> (Kahlil Gibran, quoted by Stefan Kanfer in *The New York Times Magazine*, June 25, 1972.)

HADAS' LAW
The larger and more indiscriminate the audience, the greater the need to safeguard and purify standards of quality and taste.

> (Moses Hadas, quoted in *Performing Arts*, August 1969.)

THE FIRST LAW FOR HISTORIANS
Never utter an untruth.

> (Cicero, *De Oratore*.)

THE SECOND LAW FOR HISTORIANS
Suppress nothing that is true. Moreover, there shall be no suspicion of partiality in his writing or of malice.

> (Ibid.)

THE IRON LAW OF HISTORY
No longing is completely fulfilled.

> (Henry Kissinger, then Secretary of State, quoted in *The New York Times Magazine*, October 28, 1973.)

AN IRON LAW OF HOLLYWOOD
Nothing succeeds like failure.

> (Quoted by Sidney Zion, in *New York* magazine, January 24, 1977.)

THE LAW OF HOLLYWOOD
American Revolution pictures die at the box office.
>   (*Life*, April 26, 1968.)

THE LAW OF THE INEFFICIENCY OF ART
The cost of certain cultural services (chiefly live per-
formances) will not merely rise, but climb upward at a
rate faster than the cost of most other goods and services in our society.
>   (Alvin Toffler, in *The Culture Consumers*, St.
>   Martin's Press, 1964.)

AN IRON LAW OF THE INTELLECTUAL
ESTABLISHMENT
It is better to be attacked by an establishment comrade
than to be praised by an outsider.
>   (Victor S. Navasky, in *The New York Times
>   Magazine*, March 27, 1968.)

KANFER'S LAW
As the public is deprived of oleaginous philosophy, it
makes bards from hacks or journeymen.
>   (Stefan Kanfer, in *The New York Times
>   Magazine*, June 25, 1972.)

KITMAN'S FIRST LAW OF TV
If it moves, the public will watch it.
>   (Marvin Kitman, in *You Can't Judge a Book
>   by Its Cover*, Weybright & Talley, 1970.)

KITMAN'S SECOND LAW OF TV
Pure drivel tends to drive off the screen ordinary
drivel.
>   (Ibid.)

LADD'S LAW
Can you root for the hero and heroine? Can you boo
the villain? Is the action fast and furious? If the ques-
tions can be answered "yes," grab the idea and get
into production.

> (Alan Ladd, Jr., producer of *Star Wars*,
> quoted in *The New York Times*, July 17,
> 1977.)

LINDY'S LAW
The life expectancy of a television comic is proportional to the total amount of his exposure on the
medium.

> (Quoted in *The New Republic*, June 13,
> 1964.)

A STANDING LITERARY LAW
If a novelist has only one story, it should be a Very
Important Story, and each time he tells it, it should be
exceedingly better than the last.

> (David Royster Bates, in *Pearl Magazine*,
> The University of Texas, March 1976.)

A LITERARY GRESHAM'S LAW
To get shocks, we must go farther and farther.

> (Edwin M. Griswold, Solicitor General of
> the United States, arguing before the Su-
> preme Court, quoted in *The New York
> Times*, January 19, 1970.)

MOSTEL'S LAW
The freedom of any society varies proportionately
with the volume of its laughter.

> (Zero Mostel, quoted in *The New York
> Times*, circa 1965.)

NOSREME'S LAW
If a man can write muddier prose than his neighbor, if he can arrange words in ways that befuddle the brain and grate on the ear, he will never have to monkey with a better mousetrap.

> (Wallace Carroll, editor of *The Winston-Salem Journal & Sentinel* in *The Bulletin of the American Society of Newspaper Editors*, May 1970.)

PAGE'S LAW
The number of agency people required to shoot a commercial on location is in direct proportion to the mean temperature of the location.

> (Shelby H. Page, quoted in *The New York Times*, July 14, 1968.)

THE LAW OF PLACE
All the best seats are reserved for the classes who have the most money.

> (Juvenal, in "Against the City of Rome," quoted in *The New York Times*, September 24, 1970.)

POPE'S LAW
All looks yellow to a jaundiced eye.

> (Alexander Pope, quoted by Laurence J. Peter, in *Peter's Quotations*, William Morrow, 1977.)

THE LAW OF RASPBERRY JAM
The wider a culture is spread, the thinner it must become.

> (Alvin Toffler, quoting and disagreeing with Stanley Edgar Hyman in *The Culture Consumers*.)

THE THIRD LAW OF REVIEWER EMOTION
To every action there is always an equal and opposite, or contrary, reaction.

> (John Leonard, in *The New York Times Book Review*, June 10, 1973.)

SEGEL'S LAW
The more a collector's item is promoted as an investment, the less likely it is to be a good investment. Conversely, the less an item is promoted as an investment, the more likely it is to become a good investment.

> (Joseph M. Segel, chairman of the Franklin Mint, quoted in *The National Observer*, December 23, 1972.)

AN IRON LAW OF SHOW BUSINESS
The greater the hit, the louder the distractions.

> (*Time*, November 23, 1970.)

THE FIRST LAW OF SHOW BUSINESS
INTERCOURSE
Never say never.

> (Elia Kazan, in *The Understudy*, Stein and Day, 1975.)

SLONIMSKY'S LAW
It takes approximately 20 years to make an artistic curiosity of a modernist monstrosity and another 20 years to make it a masterpiece.

> (Nicolas Slonimsky, in *Lexicon of Musical Invective*, quoted in *The New York Times Book Review*, 1969.)

WARHOL'S LAW
In the future, everybody will be famous for at least
fifteen minutes.

> (Andy Warhol, quoted in *Time*, June 19,
> 1978.)

WHITTEMORE'S LAW
Judgment in literature is impugned to the extent that
it is exercised.

> (Reed Whittemore, in *The New Republic*,
> May 2, 1970.)

FLIP WILSON'S FIRST LAW OF HUMOR
Things can be funny only when we are in fun. When
we are in "dead earnest," humor is the thing that is
dead.

> (Flip Wilson, quoted in *The New York
> Times*, July 17, 1968.)

FLIP WILSON'S LAWS OF COMEDY
Be sudden, be neat. Be unimpassioned. If you are
serious about something, leave it out.

> (Flip Wilson, quoted in *Time*, January 31,
> 1972.)

CHAPTER FIVE

THE LAWS OF ECONOMICS

THUS IS THE PROBLEM OF
RICH AND POOR TO BE SOLVED.
THE LAW OF ACCUMULATION
WILL BE LEFT FREE;
THE LAWS OF DISTRIBUTION FREE.
INDIVIDUALISM WILL CONTINUE,
BUT THE MILLIONAIRE WILL BE
BUT A TRUSTEE OF THE POOR;
ENTRUSTED FOR A SEASON
WITH A GREAT PART
OF THE INCREASED WEALTH
OF THE COMMUNITY,
BUT ADMINISTERING IT
FOR THE COMMUNITY FAR BETTER
THAN IT WOULD HAVE DONE
FOR ITSELF.
Andrew Carnegie

BECKER'S LAW
It is much easier to find a job than to keep one.
> (Jules Becker, quoted by Alan L. Otten, in
> *The Wall Street Journal*, March 14, 1974.)

THE BENIGN DEMOGRAPHIC TRANSITION
The way to reduce fertility is to shower poor people
with food and wealth; zero population will then au-
tomatically ensue.
> (Quoted by Garrett Hardin, in *BioScience*,
> July 1975.)

BRILOFF'S LAW
Whenever ants swarm, the pot will not only contain a
bit of honey, but will also be filled with accounting
gimmicks.
> (Abraham J. Briloff, in *Unaccountable Ac-
> counting*, Harper & Row, 1972.)

BUCHWALD'S LAW
As the economy gets better, everything else gets
worse.
> (Art Buchwald, quoted in *Time*, January 31,
> 1972.)

BUTZ'S LAW
When farm prices go up, they usually come down
later. But when other prices go up, they usually stay
up.
> (Earl Butz, quoted in a *New York Times*
> editorial, September 8, 1973.)

AN ABSOLUTE LAW OF CAPITALISM
Uneven economic and political development is an

absolute law of capitalism. Hence, the victory of socialism is possible first in a few or even one single capitalist country.

> (V. I. Lenin, 1870—1924.)

AN IRON LAW OF CAPITALISM
The greater the reward in view, the greater the risk.

> (Quoted by Dan Dorfman, in *New York* magazine, December 2, 1974.)

THE FIRST LAW OF ECONOMICS
There is no such thing as a free lunch.

> (Quoted by Burton Crane, in *The Sophisticated Investor*, Simon and Schuster, 1959, but also attributed to the University of Chicago school of economists by Paul Samuelson, in *Newsweek*, December 29, 1969.)

SOME EGGERS LAWS ON DOING BUSINESS WITH A FRENCHMAN
Whereas the American tries to think in a straight line, the Frenchman insists on thinking in a circle.

A French businessman mistrusts the very things in which an American businessman has the most confidence.

An American businessman tends to forget what he's said in a letter. A French businessman never forgets what he's purposely left out.

An American will probably lose his typical enthusiasm for a project before a Frenchman gets over his typical reservations.

A French company prepares its balance sheet and profit and loss statement not to show its stockholders how much money it has made, but to show the tax authorities how little.

A Frenchman feels as ill at ease with anything mechanical as an American does with a domestic servant.

An American treats his company like a wife; a Frenchman treats each of his companies like a mistress.

> (E. Russell Eggers, in *Harper's*, August 1965.)

THE EXECUTIVE UMBRELLA LAW
A businessman needs three umbrellas—one to leave at the office, one to leave at home and one to leave on the train.

> (Quoted by Paul Dickson, in *Playboy*, April 1978.)

THE FIRST LAW OF EXPERT ADVICE
Don't ask a barber if you need a haircut.

> (Daniel Greenberg, quoted by Alan L. Otten, in *The Wall Street Journal*, September 18, 1977.)

THE FIRST LAW OF FORECASTING
Forecasting is very difficult, especially if it's about the future.

> (Quoted by Alan L. Otten, in *The Wall Street Journal*, September 18, 1977.)

GRESHAM'S LAW
When two coins are equal in debt-paying value but unequal in intrinsic value, the one having the lesser intrinsic value tends to remain in circulation and the other to be hoarded or exported.

Or, more frequently, bad money drives out the good.

> (Sir Thomas Gresham, 1519–1579.)

KERNS' LAW
A college graduate's chances of obtaining a job stand in inverse proportion to the length of his hair.

> (John Kerns, quoted in *Newsweek*, July 5, 1971.)

LANSKY'S LAW
If you have a lot of what people want and can't get, then you can supply the demand and shovel in the dough.

> (Meyer Lansky, quoted by Martin A. Gosch and Richard Hammer, in *The Last Testament of Lucky Luciano*, Little, Brown, 1975.)

LEONTIEF'S LAW
New scientific knowledge is like wine in the wedding of Cana: it cannot be used up; the same idea can serve many users simultaneously; and as the number of customers increases, no one need be getting less of it because the others are getting more.

LEONTIEF'S PARADOX
In the United States, capital rather than labor is the relatively scarce factor of production.

> (Wassily Leontief, quoted in *The New York Times*, October 19, 1973.)

LEVIN'S LAW
Stocks do not move unless they are pushed.

> (S. Jay Levin, in a letter to *The New York Times*, December 19, 1971.)

MALTHUS' LAW
That population does invariably increase where there
are means of subsistence, the history of every people
that have ever existed will abundantly prove.
Or, more commonly, poverty and distress are un-
avoidable, since population increases by a geometric
ratio and the means of subsistence by arithmetic ratio.
>   (Thomas Malthus, 176–1834.)

THE LAW OF THE MARKETPLACE
Change or perish.
>   (Robert B. Walker, quoted in *The New
>   Yorker*, December 19, 1970.)

MASLOW'S RULE
The closer a need comes to being satisfied, the larger
an increment of additional gratification will be required to produce the same satisfaction.
>   (Quoted by Marshall McLuhan, in *The New
>   York Times*, September 21, 1974.)

MEYER'S LAWS OF ADVERTISING
1. Bad shops tend to get worse and good ones to get
   better.
2. The name acquires the attributes of the thing, not
   vice versa.
3. Years on the job have little to do with experience.
4. The youthful viewpoint has little to do with age.
5. Any bright tyro can write a great national campaign; only an old pro can write a good brochure.
6. The less able a person is to create advertising himself, the more likely he is to make changes in the
   art or copy if he has authority to do so.
7. Secure people share credit; insecure people steal
   it.

8. Doubling the work load does not double the work.
9. It is better to work for a smart son of a bitch than for a dumb son of a bitch.
10. The best ad is a good product.
> (Alan H. Meyer, in *Marketing/Communications*, August 1970.)

THE SEVEN LAWS OF MONEY
1. Money will come when you are doing the right thing.
2. Money has its own rules, records, budgets, savings, borrowings.
3. Money is a dream: a fantasy as alluring as the Pied Piper.
4. Money is a nightmare: in jail, robbery, fears of poverty.
5. You can never really give money away.
6. You can never really receive money as a gift.
7. There are worlds without money.
> (Michael Phillips, in *The Seven Laws of Money*, Word Wheel and Random House, 1974.)

NEILL'S THEORY OF CONTRARY OPINION
The public is almost always wrong at any major turning point in the economy or the stock market.
> (Humphrey B. Neill, quoted by Sylvia Porter, in *The New York Post*, December 29, 1969.)

THE PAPER LAW
A nation's standard of living can be measured by the amount of paper it uses, and in the U.S. we consume a record high quantity of paper.
> (Sign in the Franklin Institute Museum in Philadelphia.)

PARETO'S LAW
Every society has about the same degree of inequality; there is really very little that governments can do to alter this.

> (Vilfredo Pareto, quoted by Paul A. Samuelson, in *Newsweek*, December 17, 1973.)

THE LAW OF PETROLEUM
Where there are Muslims, there is oil; the converse is not true.

> (Charles Issawi, in *The Columbia Forum*, Summer 1970.)

POPE'S FIRST LAW OF MUTUAL FUNDS
Exceptionally high profit performance is accompanied by rates of new money that are too high to be sustained indefinitely.

POPE'S SECOND LAW OF MUTUAL FUNDS
New money does more to determine good performance than good performance does to attract new money.

> (Alan Pope, quoted in *Fortune*, June 1, 1968.)

POWELL'S LAW
The demand for "free" (i.e., taxpayer paid) health care is infinite, and would not be met even by using a country's entire gross national product.

> (Enoch Powell, quoted by Harry Schwartz, in *The New York Times*, March 26, 1975.)

ROCHE'S LAW OF LEGAL EMPLOYMENT
The chief priority for any government that hopes to achieve stability is to provide full employment for lawyers.

> (John P. Roche, in *The Albany Times-Union*, February 20, 1970.)

ROSTEN'S LAWS
1. Thinking is harder work than hard work.
2. The love of money is the source of an enormous amount of good; the fact that the good is a by-product of the selfish pursuit of riches has nothing to do with its indisputable value.
3. Most people confuse complexity with profundity; and opaque prose with deep meaning. But the greatest ideas have been expressed clearly.
4. Most men never mature; they simply grow taller.

> (Leo Rosten, quoted in *The Saturday Review*, April 4, 1970.)

SAY'S LAW
The demand for products is equal to the sum of the products in a capitalist society; thus a nation always has the means of buying all it produces; and thus overproduction is impossible.

> (Jean Baptiste Say, 1767–1832.)

SHULTZ'S LAW
Price controls work best when they are needed least.

> (George P. Shultz, quoted in *The New York Times*, January 10, 1973.)

STEWART'S LAW
Three years of bad results is invariably followed by three years of worse losses.

> (George Stewart, quoted in *The New York Times*, October 30, 1963.)

SUTTON'S LAW
Q: "Why do you rob banks?"
A: "That's where the money is."

> (Attributed to Willie Sutton, who on *Sixty Minutes* on August 8, 1976, denied he had said it.)

TURNER'S THIRD LAW OF HOUSING
Deficiencies and imperfections in your housing are infinitely more tolerable if they are your responsibility than somebody else's.

> (John Turner, quoted by Martin Mayer, in *The Builders*, W. W. Norton, 1978.)

WOODRUFF'S IRON LAW
The grandest mansion any robber baron ever built cannot stand if the land is suitable for an office building, a department store or even a very large apartment house.

> (A.M. Woodruff, quoted in *The Builders*.)

CHAPTER SIX

THE LAWS OF GOVERNMENT

GOOD LAWS
LEAD TO THE MAKING
OF BETTER LAWS;
BAD LAWS
BRING ABOUT WORSE.
Jean Jacques Rousseau

LORD ACTON'S LAW
Power tends to corrupt, and absolute power corrupts
absolutely.
>   (Lord Acton, 1834–1902, in a letter, 1887.)

BOHLEN'S LAW
What's public is propaganda, what's secret is serious.
>   (Charles Bohlen, quoted by Max Lerner, in
>   *The New York Post,* March 31, 1969.)

FIRST LAW OF MUNICIPAL BUDGETING
Every authorized job line must be filled.
>   (Francis X. Clines, in *The New York Times,*
>   February 2, 1976.)

CARTER'S LAW
The bar serves too few of the many and protects too
many of the few, including lawyers.
>   (Jimmy Carter, quoted in a *New York Times*
>   editorial, May 6, 1978.)

COHEN'S LAW
Everyone knows that the name of the game is what
label you succeed in imposing on the facts.
>   (Jerome Cohen, quoted in *Malice in Blun-
>   derland,* by Thomas L. Martin, Jr.,
>   McGraw-Hill, 1973.)

THE DEWEY THEORY
It is good to be hated by the hated.
>   (Attributed to Thomas E. Dewey, by
>   Stewart Alsop, in *Newsweek,* November
>   24, 1969.)

DU PONT'S RULES OF LEGISLATING
1. The speed at which the legislative process seems to work is in inverse proportion to your enthusiasm for the bills.
2. The title of bills, like those of Marx Brothers' movies, often have little to do with their substance.

> (Pierre Du Pont, quoted by Alan L. Otten, in *The Wall Street Journal*, September 18, 1977.)

THE DUPRÉEL THEOREM
In conflict, the character and actions of the "aggressor" and the "defender" soon tend to mirror one another.

> (Quoted by C. W. Maynes in *The New York Times*, July 25, 1973.)

THE IRON LAW OF EMULATION
Whenever any branch of government acquires a new technique which enhances its power in relation to other branches, that technique will soon be adopted by those other branches as well.

> (Daniel P. Moynihan, in *Commentary*, June 1978.)

THE LAW OF ESCALATING EXTREMISM
No matter how radical a group may be, it will soon run into a more radical opposition once it assumes power.

> (*The New York Times*, in an editorial, April 13, 1971.)

FINLEY'S LAW
There is one universal law applicable to all tyrants,

absolute monarchs and despots, enlightened or otherwise, and that is that they need not obey the prevailing rules of their societies regarding marriage and the family.

> (M. I. Finley, in *The Listener*, December 3, 1964.)

THE FLYE AMENDMENT TO LORD ACTON
If power corrupts, being out of power corrupts absolutely.

> (Douglass Cater, in *Dana: The Irrelevant Man*, McGraw-Hill, 1970.)

A LAW OF FOREIGN POLICYMAKING
The number of available options and the room for freedom of choice are usually even more limited than in domestic affairs.

> (Walter Z. Laqueur, in *Commentary*, March 1977.)

FRANKEL'S LAW
Whatever happens in government could have happened differently, and it usually would have been better if it had.

> (Charles Frankel, in *High on Foggy Bottom*, Harper & Row, 1970.)

GALBRAITH'S LAW
The more underdeveloped the country, the more overdeveloped the women.

> (John Kenneth Galbraith, quoted in *Time*, October 17, 1969.)

GALBRAITH'S FOURTH LAW OF POLITICAL WISDOM
Anyone who says he isn't going to resign four times, definitely will.

> (John Kenneth Galbraith, quoted in *The New York Times*, November 7, 1973.)

GOLDSCHMIDT'S LAW
In any United Nations forum, the least important political issue drives out the most important economic issue.

> (Arthur E. Goldschmidt, quoted in *The New York Times*, February 23, 1969.)

A LAW OF GOVERNING
He who makes the speech makes the policy; at least, he tries to.

> (Elizabeth Drew in *The New Yorker*, May 1, 1978.)

AN IRON LAW OF GOVERNMENT
The more government tampers with the daily lives of its citizens, the less authority it ends up having.

> (Stephen Miller, in *Commentary*, March 1977.)

GUMMIDGE'S LAW
The amount of expertise varies in inverse proportion to the number of statements understood by the general public.

> (*Time*, December 30, 1966.)

THE GUPPY LAW
When outrageous expenditures are divided finely enough, the public will not have enough stake in any one expenditure to squelch it.

> (Fred Reed, in *Federal Times*, June 27, 1978.)

HACKER'S LAW
The belief that enhanced understanding will necessarily stir a nation (or an organization) to action is one of mankind's oldest illusions.

> (Andrew Hacker, in *The End of an American Era*, quoted in *Malice in Blunderland*.)

HANNAFORD'S FIRST LAW OF POLITICS
In this country, all the right things get done for the wrong reasons.

> (Ben Hannaford, fictional President of the United States, in *The President*, by Drew Pearson, Doubleday, 1970.)

THE LAW OF HIGH NONSENSE
Public looniness ascends in inverse proportion to the possibility of stopping it in its tracks; or, more simply, the bigger the mess, the less the redress.

> (*The New Yorker*, June 29, 1968.)

HIMMELFARB'S LAW
Liberty too can corrupt, and absolute liberty can corrupt absolutely.

> (Gertrude Himmelfarb, in *On Liberty and Liberalism: The Case of John Stuart Mill*, Alfred A. Knopf, 1974, quoted in *Newsweek*, August 12, 1974.)

THE LAW OF HISTORICAL LESSONS
Those who don't study the past will repeat its errors;
those who do study it will find other ways to err.

> (Charles Wolf, Jr., quoted by Alan L. Ot-
> ten, in *The Wall Street Journal*, February 26,
> 1976.)

THE FIRST LAW OF INTERNATIONAL AQUATICS
It is very uncomfortable to be in a bathtub with an
elephant.

> (Barbara Ward, quoted in *The New York
> Times*, May 29, 1968.)

INTERNATIONAL CONFERENCE LAW NO. 1
Protocol and the fine points of procedure are in-
exhaustible when you want to temporize.

> (Quoted by Paul Hofmann, in *The New
> York Times*, December 2, 1968.)

AN IRON LAW OF INTERNATIONAL NEGOTIATIONS
Progress is inversely related to comfort.

> (Chester L. Cooper, in *The New York Times*,
> September 8, 1975.)

THE IRON LAW OF INCREMENTALISM
If a wise policymaker proceeds through a succession
of incremental changes, he avoids serious lasting mistakes in several ways.

> (Charles E. Lindbloom in *The Science of
> Muddling Through*, quoted by Daniel P.
> Moynihan, in *The New York Times*, January
> 12, 1970.)

JUHANI'S LAW
The compromise will always be more expensive than
either of the suggestions it is compromising.

> (Quoted in *Murphy's Law*, by Arthur
> Bloch, Price/Stern/Sloan, 1977.)

KOROLOGOS' FIRST LAW
When 51 Senators tell you that they're against a bill or
nomination, but assure you it will pass anyway,
you're in trouble.

> (Tom C. Korologos, quoted in *Newsweek*,
> December 27, 1971.)

LAL'S LAW
Things are always getting better and worse in India at
the same time.

> (Purushottam Lal, quoted in *The New York
> Times Magazine*, April 4, 1976.)

MC CLAUGHRY'S LAW OF ZONING
Where zoning is not needed, it will work perfectly;
where it is desperately needed, it always breaks
down.

> (John McClaughry, quoted by Alan L. Ot-
> ten, in *The Wall Street Journal*, February 20,
> 1975.)

MEYER'S LAW
If the facts don't fit the theory, discard the facts.

> (Quoted by C. L. Sulzberger, in *The New
> York Times*, August 20, 1969.)

MOBIL'S MURPHY'S LAW
Bad regulation begets worse regulation.
> (Ad by the Mobil Oil Corporation quoted
> by Alan L. Otten, in *The Wall Street Journal*,
> February 20, 1977.)

THE FIRST LAW OF NATIONS
In an emergency, the government will do what is
necessary to protect what is necessary.
> (George F. Will, in *Newsweek*, February 6,
> 1978.)

OTTEN'S LAW
The length of a country's national anthem is inversely
proportional to the importance of the country.
> (Alan L. Otten, in a letter to the author,
> April 1, 1968.)

OTTEN'S LAW OF TESTIMONY
When a person says that in the interest of saving time,
he will summarize his prepared testimony, he will
talk only three times as long as if he had read the
statement in the first place.
> (Alan L. Otten, in *The Wall Street Journal*,
> February 26, 1976.)

THE FIRST LAW OF THE PRESIDENCY
Almost every decision divides.
> (James Reston, in *The New York Times*,
> January 23, 1977.)

REEDY'S LAW
Isolation from reality is inseparable from the exercise of power.

> (George M. Reedy, in "Problems of Isolation in the Presidency," quoted in *The Imperial Presidency*, by Arthur Schlesinger, Jr., Houghton Mifflin, 1973.)

ROCHE'S LAW
Those who can conspire haven't got the time; those who do conspire haven't got the talent.

> (John P. Roche, quoted in *Time*, January 12, 1968.)

THE RULE OF 2½
Any military project will take twice as long as planned, cost twice as much and produce only half of what is needed.

> (Attributed to Cyrus Vance, then Undersecretary of Defense, quoted by Alan L. Otten, in *The Wall Street Journal*, December 20, 1973.)

SCHLESINGER'S UNCERTAINTY PRINCIPLE
Given the poverty of formal systems techniques to handle the unknowable facts, the decision-maker should adopt the informal procedure of "informed procrastination."

> (James C. Schlesinger, quoted in *The New York Times*, July 30, 1973.)

STROUT'S LAW
There is a major scandal in American political life every 50 years: Grant's in 1873, Teapot Dome in 1923,

Watergate in 1973. Nail down your seats for 2023.
> (Richard Strout, quoted in *Time*, March 27, 1978.)

SYMINGTON'S LAW
For every credibility gap, there is a gullibility gap.
> (Stuart Symington, quoted by Ann Landers, in *The Poughkeepsie Journal*, March 26, 1978.)

TUCHMAN'S LAW (1)
If power corrupts, weakness in the seat of power, with its constant necessity of deals and bribes and corporation arrangements, corrupts even more.
> (Barbara Tuchman, quoted by Laurence J. Peter, in *Peter's Quotations*, William Morrow, 1977.)

WICKER'S LAW
Government expands to absorb revenue, and then some.
> (Tom Wicker, in *The New York Times*, June 7, 1964.)

CHAPTER SEVEN

THE LAWS OF THE MEDIA

THE PRESENT IS BIG
WITH THE FUTURE,
THE FUTURE MIGHT BE READ
IN THE PAST,
THE DISTANT IS EXPRESSED
IN THE NEAR.
Leibniz's Law of Continuity

THE LAW OF EDITORIAL CORRECTION
Anyone nit-picking enough to write a letter of correction to an editor doubtless deserves the error that
provoked it.

> (Alvin Toffler, in a letter to *The New York
> Times Magazine*, March 18, 1968.)

THE EDITORIAL WRITER'S DISEASE
The victim comes to feel that once he has stated a
problem clearly, and told how it should be solved—
which is usually easy when you don't have the responsibility for actually carrying out the
amelioration—things are somehow better.

> (Bruce Bliven, former editor of *The New
> Republic*, in *The New Republic*, January 9,
> 1971.)

A NEW LAW OF EGO
The fury engendered by the misspelling of a name in a
column is in direct proportion to the obscurity of the
person mentioned.

> (Alan Deitz, quoted by Alan L. Otten, in
> *The Wall Street Journal*, September 18,
> 1977.)

EMERSON'S LAW
If a man can write a better book, preach a better
sermon, or make a better mousetrap than his
neighbor, though he builds his house in the wilderness, the world will make a beaten path to his door.

> (Ralph Waldo Emerson, quoted by Wallace
> Carroll, in the *Bulletin of the American Soci-
> ety of Newspaper Editors*, May 1970.)

FABER'S SECOND LAW
The number of errors in any piece of writing rises in
direct proportion to the writer's reliance on secondary
sources.

> (Harold Faber, in *The New York Times
> Magazine*, April 7, 1968.)

GERMOND'S LAW
When a group of newsmen go out for dinner together,
the bill is to be divided equally among them, regardless of what each one drinks and eats.

> (Jack Germond, then of the Gannett pap-
> ers, later deputy managing editor of *The
> Washington Star*.)

GUNTHER'S FIRST LAW
Never take notes on both sides of the paper.

GUNTHER'S SECOND LAW
All happiness depends on a leisurely breakfast.

> (John Gunther, journalist and author,
> quoted in *Newsweek*, June 8, 1970.)

HOOKER'S LAW OF JOURNALISM
He that goeth about to persuade a multitude that they
are not so well governed as they ought to be, shall
never want for attentive or favorable hearers
.... whereas on the other side, if we maintain things
that are established we have to strive with a number of
heavy prejudices in the hearts of men who think that
herein we serve the time and speak in favor of the
present state because thereby we either hold or see
preferment.

> (Bishop Richard Hooker, 1554−1600,
> quoted by Theodore H. White, in *The Mak-
> ing of the President 1972*, Atheneum, 1973.)

JOHNSON'S THIRD LAW
If you miss one issue of any magazine, it will be the
issue which contained the article, story or installment
you were most anxious to read.

>（Quoted in *Murphy's Law*, by Arthur Bloch,
>Price/Stern/Sloan, 1977.)

THE FIRST LAW OF JOURNALISM (1)
To confirm existing prejudice, rather than contradict
it.

>(Alexander Cockburn, in *More*, May 1974.)

THE FIRST LAW OF JOURNALISM (2)
Any official denial is de facto a confirmation.

>(John Kifner, in *The New York Times*, June
>29, 1969.)

KENNEDY'S LAW
Excessive official restraints on information are invariably self-defeating and productive of headaches for
the officials concerned.

>(Edward Kennedy, the AP correspondent
>who broke the news of the armistice at the
>end of World War II, quoted by Gladwin
>Hill, in *The New York Times Magazine*, July
>27, 1969.)

THE FIRST LAW OF LEAK PHYSICS
Leaks tend to follow the source of greatest impact.

>(Robert Sherrill, in *The New York Times*,
>January 9, 1972.)

THE LINDLEY RULE
FOR WASHINGTON CORRESPONDENTS
This report is presented solely on my authority, and readers will just have to assume and believe that I haven't made it up out of nothing.

> (Ernest Lindley, quoted by William Safire, in *The New Language of Politics*, Random House, 1968.)

LIPPMANN'S LAW OF JOURNALISM
There can be no higher law in journalism than to tell the truth and shame the devil....Remain detached from the great.

> (Walter Lippmann, quoted by Anthony Lewis, in *The New York Times*, February 26, 1974.)

MARCUS' LAW
The number of letters written to the editor is inversely proportional to the importance of the article.

> (Robert L. Marcus, in a letter to *The New York Times Magazine*, April 17, 1968.)

O'BRIEN'S PRINCIPLE
Auditors always reject any expense account with a bottom line dividable by five or ten.

> (Emmett O'Brien of the Gannett papers, quoted by Alan L. Otten, in *The Wall Street Journal*, March 14, 1974.)

OTTEN'S LAW OF TYPESETTING
Typesetters always correct intentional errors, but always fail to correct unintentional ones.

> (Alan L. Otten, in *The Wall Street Journal*, February 20, 1975.)

THE NEW PETER PRINCIPLE
Poets want the price of their books to be so low that other poets and the public can afford them, but on the other hand also want a substantial advance for their work.

> (Peter Davison, quoted in *The New York Times Book Review*, November 16, 1975.)

THE (HAGERTY) LAW OF PRESS SECRETARIES
If you lose your temper at a newspaper columnist, he'll get rich or famous or both.

> (James C. Hagerty, quoted by Robert Donovan, in *The New York Journal-American*, March 25, 1964.)

THE (ROSS) LAW OF PRESS SECRETARIES
Never characterize the importance of a statement in advance.

> (Charles G. Ross, quoted by Donovan, ibid.)

THE (SALINGER) LAW OF PRESS SECRETARIES
Quit when you're still behind.

> (Pierre Salinger, quoted by Donovan, ibid.)

THE SECOND LAW OF PUBLO-DYNAMICS
There's nothing like a text with bylines to assure anonymity.

> (John Kenneth Galbraith, quoted in *The New York Times*, August 17, 1971.)

SAFIRE'S COROLLARY TO PARKINSON'S LAW
News expands to fill the time and space allocated to its coverage.

> (William Safire, in *The New York Times*, September 6, 1973.)

TUCHMAN'S LAW (2)
The fact of being reported increases the apparent extent of a deplorable development by a factor of ten.

> (Barbara Tuchman, in *The Atlantic*, September 1973.)

VAN NORTWICK'S FORMULA
When your name appears in public print, the persons you would like to see it are out of town and do not read the paper that day.

VAN NORTWICK'S COROLLARY
The people who do see it and call you up are the ones you least want to hear from.

> (William Buchwalter Van Nortwick, quoted by Alan L. Otten, in *The Wall Street Journal*, September 18, 1977.)

WEAVER'S LAW
Whenever several newspapermen share a cab, the person in the front seat always pays.

> (Warren Weaver of *The New York Times*, quoted in *The Wall Street Journal*, December 12, 1973.)

DOYLE'S COROLLARY TO WEAVER'S LAW
No matter how many reporters share a cab and no matter who pays, each puts the full fare on his expense account.

> (Edward P. Doyle, quoted by Alan L. Otten, in *The Wall Street Journal*, March 14, 1974.)

CHAPTER EIGHT

THE LAWS OF POLITICS

THE DENIAL THAT
MAN MAY BE ARBITRARY
IN HUMAN TRANSITION
IS THE HIGHER LAW.
BY THIS HIGHER LAW,
ALL FORMAL LAWS AND
ALL POLITICAL BEHAVIOR
ARE JUDGED IN
CIVILIZED SOCIETIES.
Walter Lippmann

ALLEN'S LAW OF POLITICO-MARKET CYCLES
Stock prices always rise in the third year of a President's administration.

> (George E. Allen, quoted in *Time*, February 15, 1971.)

THE CHAPPAQUIDDICK THEOREM
There is no time for a political figure to tell bad news except right away. The longer a political leader waits to put forth his bad news, the worse will be the effect.

> (James Doyle, quoted in Theodore H. White's *Breach of Faith*, Atheneum, 1975.)

THE LAW OF CLEAR BLUE WATER
For poll evidence to be of value to an underdog candidate, the evidence must be massive and uncontradictable; there must be clear blue water between the underdog and the favorite, say 10 percentage points.

> (Richard M. Scammon and Ben J. Wattenberg, in *The Real Majority*, Coward McCann, 1970.)

EVANS' LAW OF POLITICS
When our people get to the point where they can do us some good, they stop being our people.

> (M. Stanton Evans, quoted by Alan L. Otten, in *The Wall Street Journal*, February 20, 1975.)

FARLEY'S LAW
People make up their minds by summer how to vote.

> (James A. Farley, quoted by Jules Abels, in *Out of the Jaws of Victory*, Holt, 1959.)

FISCHER'S LAW
In American politics, nothing much happens until the status quo becomes more painful than change.
> (John Fischer, in *Vital Signs, U.S.A.* Harper & Row, 1975.)

GALBRAITH'S FIRST LAW OF POLITICS
The professionals in both parties will always prefer the poorest man that the electorate will be persuaded to accept and will invariably exaggerate their persuasive powers.
> (John Kenneth Galbraith, in *New York* magazine, November 15, 1971.)

JORDAN'S LAW
Every New Mexico citizen stands foursquare for everyone else paying his fair share.
> (Robert Jordan, quoted in *The Wall Street Journal*, January 12, 1972.)

KNEBEL'S SECOND LAW OF POLITICS
A candidate for re-election will do anything to insure victory.

KNEBEL'S FIRST LAW OF POLITICS
That law number 2 takes precedence over all others.
> (Fletcher Knebel, in *Vanished*, Doubleday, 1968.)

THE LEGUM LAW OF INHERENT OPPOSITES
A candidate always says the opposite of what he means and predicts the opposite of what he thinks will occur.
> (David Broder, in *The Washington Post*, 1967.)

MC CRACKEN'S LAW
There is some kind of malevolent law about the
rhythm of politics that puts Republicans in charge of
the United States government when it is hard to be a
hero.

> (Paul W. McCracken, quoted in *The New
> York Times*, September 16, 1970.)

MANKIEWICZ'S SECOND LAW OF POLITICS
A politician will tip off his true belief by stating the
opposite at the beginning of a sentence. For maximum
comprehension, do not start listening until the first
clause is concluded; begin at the word "but" which
begins the second—or active—clause.

> (Frank Mankiewicz, quoted by Alan L. Ot-
> ten, in *The Wall Street Journal*, February 26,
> 1976.)

MENCKEN'S LAW
Never overestimate the intelligence of the voter.

> (H. L. Mencken, quoted in *The New York
> Times*, February 18, 1968.)

MOSHER'S LAW
It usually is a mistake for anyone in public office to
seek re-election after age 70.

> (Charles A. Mosher, in *The New York
> Times*, January 15, 1976.)

MUGGERIDGE'S LAW
If a candidate wants it too much, the convention turns
him down.

> (Malcolm Muggeridge, quoted by Stewart
> Alsop, in *Nixon and Rockefeller*, Double-
> day, 1960.)

THE IRON LAW OF OLIGARCHY
It is organization which gives birth to the domination of the elected over the electors, of delegates over the delegators. Who says organization, says oligarchy.
> (Robert Michels, the German sociologist, quoted by Victor S. Navasky, in *The New York Times Magazine*, August 25, 1969.)

A CAMPAIGN COROLLARY TO PARKINSON'S LAW
Words directed at the electorate multiply in direct proportion to the time and space available on TV and radio and in magazines and newspapers.
> (*Time*, November 8, 1968.)

THE FIRST LAW OF POLITICO-DYNAMICS
Mood determines strategy, and strategy determines candidates.
> (Max Lerner, in *The New York Post*, August 14, 1968.)

A LAW OF AMERICAN POLITICS
Nobody runs for the vice-presidential nomination.
> (Harold Faber, in *You and Elections '72*, Prentice-Hall, 1972.)

THE FIRST LAW OF POLITICS (1)
You can't beat somebody with nobody.
> (William Safire, in *The New Language of Politics*, Random House, 1968.)

THE FIRST LAW OF POLITICS (2)
Get re-elected.
> (Harold Faber, in *The New York Times Magazine*, March 17, 1968.)

PRICE'S LAW OF POLITICS
It's easier to be a liberal a long way from home.
> (Don Price, quoted by Alan L. Otten, in *The Wall Street Journal*, December 20, 1973.)

RAKOVE'S FIRST LAW OF POLITICS
The amount of effort put into a campaign by a worker increases in proportion to the personal benefit he will derive from his party's victory.

RAKOVE'S LAW OF PRINCIPLE AND POLITICS
A citizen is influenced by principle in direct proportion to his distance from the political situation.
> (Milton Rakove, in the *Virginia Quarterly Review*, Summer 1965.)

RAYBURN'S LAW
When you get too big a majority, you're immediately in trouble.
> (Sam Rayburn, quoted by William Safire, in *The New York Times*, January 23, 1975.)

RAYBURN'S FIRST LAW OF POLITICS
To get along, go along.
> (Sam Rayburn, quoted by James Reston, in *The New York Times*, October 14, 1973.)

RESTON'S LAW OF POLITICS
Power creates its own resistance, and the rule of diminishing returns usually gets stronger for Presidents with every passing year.
> (James Reston, in *The New York Times*, November 27, 1966.)

RESTON'S PRACTICAL RULE OF POLITICS
When confronted by an old Congressional rascal and a
new rascal, always vote for the new, because the old
has seniority on the committees and, therefore, more
power.

> (James Reston, in *The New York Times*, June
> 16, 1968.)

ROCHE'S THIRD LAW
In politics, a straight line is the shortest distance to
disaster.

> (John P. Roche, quoted in *The Albany
> Times-Union*, July 3, 1976.)

SAYRE'S THIRD LAW OF POLITICS
Academic politics is the most vicious and bitter form
of politics because the stakes are so low.

SAYRE'S VARIANT OF THE THIRD LAW OF
POLITICS
Academic politics are the most vicious form of politics
because the fighting is over issues decided five years
earlier.

> (Wallace Sayre, quoted by Alan L. Otten, in
> *The Wall Street Journal*, December 12, 1974.)

SEARS' FIRST LAW OF POLITICS
You never do the same thing in politics twice.

> (John P. Sears, quoted in *The New York
> Times*, August 5, 1976.)

SHAFFER'S LAW
The effectiveness of a politician varies in inverse

proportion to his commitment to principle.

>> (Sam Shaffer, quoted in *Newsweek*, September 13, 1971.)

THE POLITICAL LAW OF SIMULTANEOUS BUT CONTRARY TRUTHS.

It is tempting to say that American politics and elections are so inexact and complex that they are perhaps the only field of human endeavor in which all the stated opinions are correct and so are their opposites.

>> (Richard M. Scammon and Ben J. Wattenberg in *The Real Majority*.)

THE SUCCABONK LAW OF POLITICS

The number of campaign promises kept is in inverse proportion to the number of campaign promises made.

>> (Alice Faber, in *The Nepperhan*, Winter 1968.)

UDALL'S FOURTH LAW OF POLITICS

If you can find something everyone agrees on, it's wrong.

>> (Morris Udall, quoted in *The New York Times*, April 4, 1975.)

WASHINGTON'S FIRST LAW OF THERMODYNAMICS

When affection for a sitting President cools down, the chatter about the senior available Kennedy heats up.

>> (*Newsweek*, May 8, 1978.)

CHAPTER NINE

THE LAWS OF SCIENCE AND TECHNOLOGY

IN THE INTERPRETATION
OF NATURAL PHENOMENA
OR SCIENTIFIC DATA,
THE SIMPLEST AND
LEAST CUMBERSOME
ASSUMPTION
IS PREFERRED.
William of Ockham

ARNEY'S LAW

Every time you come up with a great idea, you will find someone else has thought of it first.

> (Quoted in the *Farmers' Almanac*, 1978.)

BLAKE'S LAW

If there is a possibility of several things going wrong, the one that will go wrong is the one that will do the most damage.

> (Quoted in the *Farmers' Almanac*, 1978.)

CLARKE'S FIRST LAW

If an elderly but distinguished scientist says that something is possible, he is almost certainly right, but if he says that it is impossible, he is very probably wrong.

CLARKE'S SECOND LAW

The only way to find the limits of the possible is to go beyond them into the impossible.

CLARKE'S THIRD LAW

Any sufficiently advanced technology is indistinguishable from magic.

> (Arthur C. Clarke, quoted by Jeremy Bernstein, in *The New Yorker*, August 9, 1969.)

SOME LAWS OF COMPUTER PROGRAMMING

1. Any given program, when running, is obsolete.
2. Any given program costs more and takes longer.
3. If a program is useful, it will have to be changed.
4. If a program is useless, it will have to be documented.

> (Quoted in *Murphy's Law*, by Arthur Bloch, Price/Stern/Sloan, 1977.)

DOBBIN'S LAW
When in doubt, use a bigger hammer.
> (Attributed to Joe Dobbin, quoted in *Malice in Blunderland*, by Thomas L. Martin, Jr., McGraw-Hill, 1973.)

DOUGLAS' LAW
When the weight of the paperwork equals the weight of the plane, the plane will fly.
> (Donald Douglas, quoted by Alan L. Otten, in *The Wall Street Journal*, February 26, 1976.)

THE ECOLOGICAL LAW
Nobody owns anything, and all anyone has is the use of his presumed possessions.
> (Philip Wylie, in *The New York Times*, February 1, 1970.)

THE FIRST LAW OF ECOLOGY
Everything is connected to everything else.

THE SECOND LAW OF ECOLOGY
Everything must go somewhere.

THE THIRD LAW OF ECOLOGY
Nature knows best.

THE FOURTH LAW OF ECOLOGY
There is no such thing as a free lunch.
> (Barry Commoner, in *The New Yorker*, September 25, 1971.)

EDDINGTON'S THEORY
The number of different hypotheses erected to explain a given biological phenomenon is inversely proportional to the available knowledge.

(Quoted in *Murphy's Law*.)

FOUR LAWS OF ENGINEERING AND DESIGN
1. Information necessitating a change in design will be conveyed to the designer only after the plans are complete.
2. The more innocuous the revision appears at first, the farther its influence will extend with time.
3. If, when the completion of a design is imminent, field dimensions are finally supplied as they actually are instead of what they were meant to be, it is always simpler to start over.
4. Even if it is impossible to assemble a part incorrectly, a way will be found to do it wrong.

(Douglas D. Macdonald, in a letter to the author, March 18, 1968.)

THE LAW OF EVOLUTIONARY POTENTIAL
In a time of evolutionary crisis, the most backward forms of organization have the greatest potential to survive.

(Andrew Hugos, in a letter to *The New York Times Magazine*, September 14, 1974.)

FINAGLE'S LAW (1)
Once a job has been fouled up, anything done to improve it makes it worse.

(Quoted by Brooks Atkinson, in *The New York Times*, February 1, 1961.)

FINAGLE'S LAW (2)
If anything can go wrong with an experiment, it will.
> (Quoted by Gunter Cohn, in *Plating* magazine, requoting from *Product Engineering*, April 21, 1958.)

SOME GALL LAWS OF SYSTEMANTICS
New systems generate new problems.

A large system, produced by expanding the dimensions of a smaller system, does not behave like the smaller system.

A complex system designed from scratch never works and cannot be patched up to make it work. You have to start over, beginning with a simple working system.

Systems develop goals of their own the instant they come into being.

Complex systems usually work in the failure mode.

Complex systems tend to produce complex responses (not solutions) to problems.

Great advances are not produced by systems designed to produce great advances.
> (John Gall, in *Systemantics*, Quadrangle/ The New York Times Book Co., 1977.)

GILB'S LAW OF UNRELIABILITY
Computers are unreliable, but humans are even more unreliable.
> (Quoted in *Murphy's Law*.)

GUMPERSON'S LAW
The contradictory of a welcome possibility will assert
itself whenever such an eventuality is likely to be most
frustrating; or, in other words, the outcome of a de-
sired probability will be inverse to the degree of desirability.

> (Quoted in *Changing Times*, November
> 1957, and requoted in H. Allen Smith's *A
> Short History of Fingers*.)

HANHAM'S LAW
Great technological advances are always around the
corner.

> (H. J. Hanham in *Daedalus*, Spring 1971.)

THE HARVARD LAW OF ANIMAL BEHAVIOR
When all conditions are known and controlled, the
animal will behave as it damn well pleases.

> (Quoted in a letter to the author by Leigh
> Marlowe, March 19, 1968.)

HERRNSTEIN'S LAW (2)
The greater success you have in eliminating environ-
mental differences, the more clearly the genetic differences will figure.

> (Richard Herrnstein, quoted by William F.
> Buckley, Jr., in *The New York Post*, April 4,
> 1973.)

HUBBLE'S LAW
The farther away a galaxy is, the faster it moves.

> (Edwin Hubble, quoted in the *New York
> Times Magazine*, June 25, 1978.)

KELLEY'S LAW
Nothing is ever as simple as it first seems.
(Quoted in the *Farmers' Almanac*, 1978.)

KLIPSTEIN'S LAW
A patent application will be preceded by one week by a similar application made by an independent worker.
(Quoted in *Murphy's Law*.)

THE MADMAN'S RULE
Any venture into a new area of technology will cost three and a half times the original estimate because of unforeseen difficulties.
(Quoted in *The New York Times*, June 3, 1972.)

A BASIC LAW OF MEDICINE
Pills to be taken in twos always come out of the bottle in threes.
(Quoted by Alan L. Otten, in *The Wall Street Journal*, February 26, 1976.)

A MEDICAL VARIATION OF PARKINSON'S LAW
Patient admissions for surgery expand to fill beds, operating suites and surgeons' time.
(Quoted in *The New York Times*, January 27, 1976.)

THE LAW OF NEW PROCESSES
Hidden flaws are always found when you can least afford the discovery.
(Alan Deitz, quoted by Alan L. Otten, in *The Wall Street Journal*, February 26, 1976.)

NEWTON'S LAWS
1. A body at rest or in motion, if left to itself, will maintain itself in the same condition unchanged.
2. A change in the motion of a body indicates a force due to the presence of another body.
3. For every action, there is an equal and opposite reaction.

> (Sir Isaac Newton, 1642–1727.)

NEWTON'S FOURTH LAW
If I have seen further, it is by standing on the shoulders of giants.

> (Quoted in *The New York Times*, February 16, 1976.)

PARKINSON'S LAW OF MEDICAL RESEARCH
Successful research attracts the bigger grant which makes further research impossible. In accordance with this law, we mostly end as administrators.

> (C. Northcote Parkinson, in *The New Scientist*, January 25, 1962.)

PENDRED'S LAW
Successful research impedes further successful research.

> (Keith J. Pendred, in *The Bulletin of the Atomic Scientists*, March 1963.)

THE LAW OF PROGRESSIVE RETARDATION
The more progressive a project appears, the more likely it will turn out in reverse.

PERMUTATION 1
If a novel idea works, leave it alone—or at least do not expand on it.

PERMUTATION 2
Intelligent research does not guarantee the accuracy of the findings.

PERMUTATION 3
Protect your wagers by laying-off a side bet on the tortoise.

> (Robert Lincoln, in *The Financial Times*, quoted in *Atlas/World Press Review*, June 1974.)

THE THREE LAWS OF ROBOTICS
1. A robot may not injure a human being, or, through inaction, allow a human being to come to harm.
2. A robot must obey the order given it by human beings except where such orders would conflict with the First Law.
3. A robot must protect its own existence as long as such protection does not conflict with the First or Second Law.

> (*The Handbook of Robotics*, 56th edition, 2058 A.D., quoted by Isaac Asimov, in *I, Robot*, Doubleday, 1963.)

THE FIRST LAW OF SCIENTIFIC MOTIVATION
What's in it for me?

> (Quoted by Isaac Asimov, in *The Worlds of If*, December 1968.)

THE PRINCIPLE OF SCIENTIFIC PARSIMONY
If you have one explanation for a phenomenon, there is no need to seek a second explanation.
>   (George Wald, in *The New York Times*, February 29, 1976.)

SPODE'S LAW
Whenever an astronomical event takes place, a natural phenomenon obscures the event.
>   (Quoted in *The Patent Trader*, August 20, 1970.)

WATSON'S LAW (1)
The reliability of machinery is inversely proportional to the number and significance of any persons watching it.
>   (Quoted in *Murphy's Law*.)

WATSON'S LAW (2)
Nature always sides with the hidden flaw.
>   (Quoted in the *Farmers' Almanac*, 1978.)

YOUNG'S LAW
All great discoveries are made by mistake.

YOUNG'S COROLLARY
The greater the finding, the longer it takes to make the mistake.
>   (Quoted in *Murphy's Law*.)

CHAPTER TEN

THE LAWS OF SPORTS

THE CHESS BOARD IS THE WORLD,
THE PIECES ARE THE
PHENOMENA OF THE UNIVERSE,
THE RULES OF THE GAME
ARE WHAT WE CALL
THE LAWS OF NATURE.
Thomas Henry Huxley

ADE'S LAW
Anybody can win—unless there's a second entry.
> (George Ade, quoted by Laurence J. Peter,
> in *Peter's Quotations*, William Morrow,
> 1977.)

A FIRST COMMANDMENT FOR BASEBALL
MANAGERS
Thou shalt not drink in the saloons with thine ball
players.
> (Dick Young, in *The Daily News*, August
> 13, 1969.)

BERRA'S LAW
You can observe a lot just by watching.
> (Yogi Berra, quoted by Laurence J. Peter, in
> *Peter's Quotations*.)

THE FIRST LAW OF BETTING AND SEX
When I lose a football game, my wife knows I've got to
be alone; but when we win, I jump on her like a
fumble.
> (Norton Peppis, quoted by Peter Axthelm,
> in *Newsweek*, September 23, 1974.)

THE LAW OF THE BLEACHERS
First come, first served.
> (Murray Schumach, in *The New York Times*,
> October 13, 1977.)

CULBERTSON'S LAW OF SYMMETRY
An unbalanced hand and suit pattern is usually accompanied by another unbalanced one in the same

deal; the more unbalanced the distribution, the greater the chance that this will occur.

> (Ely Culbertson, quoted in *The National Observer*, December 22, 1969.)

GAINFORD'S LAW
The only thing that counts is how many behinds are in those seats.

> (George Gainford, quoted by Arthur Daley, in *The New York Times*, February 12, 1971.)

GOMEZ'S LAW
If you don't throw it, they can't hit it.

> (Lefty Gomez, quoted by Laurence J. Peter, in *Peter's Quotations*.)

KOPPETT'S LAW
Whatever creates the greatest inconvenience for the largest number must happen.

> (Leonard Koppett, in *The New York Times*, October 19, 1977.)

MURRAY'S AMENDMENT
Anything that can go to New York, will.

> (Jim Murray, quoted by Leonard Koppett, op. cit.)

LAPP'S FIRST LAW OF BASEBALL
For best offense, ground-ball hitters should bat against fly-ball yielding pitchers, and, conversely, fly-ball hitters should bat against ground-ball yielding pitchers.

LAPP'S SECOND LAW OF BASEBALL
Fly-ball yielding pitchers should be pulled, and
ground-ball yielding pitchers should be hit to the
opposite field.

> (Walter Lapp, quoted by Jim Bouton, in
> *New York* magazine, July 1, 1974.)

MEMINGER'S LAW
If you don't play ball, you can't hang out.

> (Dean Meminger, quoted in *New York*
> magazine, February 26, 1973.)

NELSON'S LAW OF MOMENTUM
If you don't make big yardage on first and second
down, you're in trouble, and if you don't think so,
you are really in trouble and you don't understand the
situation.

> (Dave Nelson, quoted in *The New York
> Times*, October 5, 1971.)

PAIGE'S LAW
Don't look back—something may be gaining on you.

> (Satchel Paige, quoted in *Time*, circa 1964.)

RUNYON'S LAW
The race is not always to the swift, nor the battle to the
strong, but that's the way to bet.

> (Damon Runyon, quoted by Laurence J.
> Peter, in *Peter's Quotations*.)

TERMAN'S LAW OF INNOVATION
If you want a track team to win the high jump, you find one person who can jump seven feet, not seven people who can jump one foot.
> (Quoted in *Murphy's Law*, by Arthur Bloch, Price/Stern/Sloan, 1977.)

WOODEN'S LAW
Repetition is the last law of learning.
> (John Wooden, quoted in *The New York Times Magazine*, December 2, 1973.)

CHAPTER ELEVEN

THE LAWS OF EVERYTHING ELSE

LIFE IS CHAOS
NOT BECAUSE THERE
ARE NO LAWS,
BUT BECAUSE THERE ARE
INNUMERABLE LAWS AND
THEY ARE CONSTANTLY
IN HAPHAZARD COLLISION.
Stephen Vicinczey

ALINSKY'S THIRD LAW OF ESTABLISHMENT-DYNAMICS

In any fight with the Establishment, you can count on it for at least one glorious gaffe that will bring renewed life to your languishing cause.

> (Saul Alinsky, quoted in *The New York Times*, March 19, 1971.)

ARENDT'S LAW OF PLURALITY

Nothing and nobody exists on this planet whose very being does not presuppose a spectator. In other words, nothing that is, insofar as it appears, exists in the singular; everything that is is meant to be perceived by somebody. Not Man, but men inhabit the earth. Plurality is the law of the earth.

> (Hannah Arendt, in *The New Yorker*, November 21, 1977.)

BUNK CARTER'S LAW

At any given time, there are more important people in the world than important jobs to contain them.

> (Attributed to Bunk Carter by Paul Crume, in *The Dallas Morning News*, quoted in *Malice in Blunderland*, by Thomas L. Martin, Jr., McGraw-Hill, 1973.)

THE LAW OF CONSERVATION OF EVIL

The total amount of evil in any system remains constant.

> (Charles Issawi, in *The Columbia Forum*, Summer 1970.)

FABER'S FIRST LAW OF HORTICULTURE
The best way to grow any crop is to put forth the least
possible effort.
>   (Doris Faber, in *The New York Times*, April
>   9, 1971.)

THE FAIL-SAFE THEOREM
When a fail-safe system fails, it fails by failing to fail
safe.
>   (John Gall, in *Systemantics*, Quadrangle/
>   The New York Times Book Co., 1977.)

FINNEGAN'S LAW
The farther away the future is, the better it looks.
>   (Quoted in *Organic Gardening*, June 1978.)

THE LAW OF HEAT
Where it is a duty to worship the sun, it is pretty sure
to be a crime to examine the laws of heat.
>   (John, Viscount Morley, 1838—1923.)

LEC'S IMMUTABLE LAW
The first requisite for immortality is death.
>   (Stanislaw J. Lec, quoted by Laurence J.
>   Peter, in *Peter's Quotations*, William Mor-
>   row, 1977.)

LYNNE'S LAW
Everything has an except in it.
>   (Quoted by Roscoe C. Born, in *The National
>   Observer*, September 5, 1970.)

MAY'S MORDANT MAXIM
A university is a place where men of principle outnumber men of honor.
>(Ernest May, quoted by Alan L. Otten, in
>*The Wall Street Journal*, December 2, 1973.)

MURPHY'S LAW
If anything can go wrong, it will.
>(Attributed to a Captain Ed Murphy of the
>Air Force by George Nicholas, quoted in
>*Murphy's Law*, by Arthur Bloch, Price/
>Stern/Sloan, 1977, but, more generally, to
>an unknown Murphy.)

MURPHY'S SECOND LAW (1)
Things go wrong in batches.
>(Phyllis Cobb, in *The Patent Trader*, Oc-
>tober 11, 1973.)

MURPHY'S SECOND LAW (2)
Nothing is ever quite as good or bad as the prevailing
mood of the moment.
>(James Reston, in *The New York Times*,
>January 22, 1978.)

MRS. MURPHY'S LAW
Anything that can go wrong will go wrong while he is
out of town.
>(Quoted by Ann Landers, in *The
>Washington Post*, May 9, 1978.)

ROYSTER'S REFINEMENT OF MURPHY'S LAW
When things go wrong anywhere, they are apt to go wrong everywhere.

> (Vermont Royster, in *The Wall Street Journal*, December 3, 1975.)

NIENBERG'S LAW
Progress is made on alternate Fridays.

> (Quoted by Paul Dickson, in *Playboy*, April 1978.)

PESIN'S LAW
When one rocks, an affirmative nod comes easily.

> (An unidentified Pesin, in *The Saturday Review*, circa 1965.)

PETER'S LAW
The unexpected always happens.

> (Laurence J. Peter, in *Peter's Quotations*.)

MS. PETER'S LAW
Today, if you are not confused, you're just not thinking clearly.

> (Irene Peter, quoted in *Peter's Quotations*.)

ROWE'S RULE
The odds are five to six that the light at the end of the tunnel is the headlight of an oncoming train.

> (Quoted by Paul Dickson, in *Playboy*, April 1978.)

STEEN'S LAW
Left to themselves, things will always go from bad to worse.

> (Quoted in the *Farmers' Almanac*, 1978.)

THE SUKHOMLINOV EFFECT
In war, victory goes to those armies whose leaders' uniforms are least impressive.

> (Named for General Sukhomlinov by Roger A. Beaumont and Bernard J. James, in *Horizon*, Winter 1971.)

TALON'S LAW
What goes up, must stay up.

> (Advertisement by the zipper company, in *The New York Times Magazine*, October 13, 1968.)

TERMAN'S LAW
There is no direct relationship between the quality of an educational program and its cost.

> (F. E. Terman, quoted in *Malice in Blunderland*.)

TODD'S LAW
Facts are not judgments, judgments are not facts.

> (Charles Todd, a fictional character in Dick Francis' *In the Frame*, Harper & Row, 1976.)

ULMANN'S RAZOR
When stupidity is a sufficient explanation, there is no need to have recourse to any other.

> (Mitchell Ulmann, quoted by Alan L. Otten, in *The Wall Street Journal*, February 26, 1976.)

WEILER'S LAW
Nothing is impossible for the man who doesn't have to do it himself.

> (A. H. Weiler, quoted in *The New York Times*, March 17, 1968.)

WEILER'S SECOND LAW
There is no such thing as a tall horizontal woman.

> (A. H. Weiler, in a privately circulated memo at *The New York Times*.)

THE WOODEN BUCKET PRINCIPLE
A tendency to imagine that almost everything in the country is simpler and more primitive and kind of nicer than it really is.

> (Noel Perrin, who warns against it, in *First Person Rural*, David R. Godine, 1978.)

And, out of order to make it appropriately the last entry in this book:

FABER'S LAW
If there isn't a law, there will be.

> (Headline over an article by Harold Faber, in *The New York Times Magazine*, March 17, 1968.)